HOW TO INVEST

Peter Stanyer is an independent investment economist. He was previously chief investment officer of a US-based wealth management firm, a managing director at Merrill Lynch, and investment director of the UK's Railways Pension Fund.

Masood Javaid was senior adviser in the managing director's office to a large sovereign wealth fund. Previously he held senior positions at Mercury Asset Management and Merrill Lynch, and managed the UK's Post Office and British Telecom pension fund assets.

Stephen Satchell is Economics Fellow at Trinity College, Cambridge. He is also Emeritus Reader in Financial Econometrics at the University of Cambridge and an honorary member of the Institute of Actuaries.

HOW TO INVEST

Navigating the brave new world of
personal investment

**Peter Stanyer, Masood Javaid and
Stephen Satchell**

Published in 2023 under exclusive licence from The Economist by
Profile Books Ltd
29 Cloth Fair
London EC1A 7JQ
www.profilebooks.com

A CIP catalogue record for this book is available from the British Library

ISBN 978 1 80081 460 8
eISBN 978 1 80081 461 5

Typeset in Milo by MacGuru Ltd

Printed and bound in Great Britain by CPI Group (UK) Ltd, Croydon CR0 4YY

Contents

Words and phrases that appear in **bold** within the text are explained in the Glossary on pages 207–21.

Introduction: We're all investors now

"MY FATHER CALLS ME LAST WEEK. 'I need your help, son. My golf buddies have been trading Robinhood. I just opened an account. What do I buy?'"[1]

Robinhood, a low cost and user-friendly online stock trading platform, was a high-profile US success story from the early days of the covid-19 pandemic when it made an impressive leap towards its avowed mission to "democratize finance for all".

Most new investors on retail trading platforms do not have a smart financial adviser in the family to ask for guidance. Instead, during the pandemic large numbers tuned in to social media. In 2020, Robinhood and its competitors spawned the phenomenon of the crowd-promoted "meme stock". This was the name given to equities that attracted followers on social media leading to widespread purchases, with apparently little attention to the reasonableness of the price being paid.

Easy to use, instantly available, inexpensive stock trading platforms have become an unmissable feature of personal investing in recent years. But how do new investors decide to what to buy and how much? And should they join the reported 100 million-plus worldwide who have ventured into buying cryptocurrencies, and if so, which cryptocurrencies? These are archetypal 21st-century investment challenges for individual investors. This book provides signposts to help steer though the fog, and sometimes the excitement, that clouds the way through.

It is easy to miss how fast the world of personal investing has changed. Love it or loathe it or just not interested in it, tens of millions are now directly involved in investment markets to a degree not known by earlier generations. This includes many millions who now have personal pension accounts and personal responsibility for pension savings and their retirement income in a way that was largely unknown in the last century. The shift of financial accountability from employers to employees has been breathtaking. Many, though, have probably gone with the flow and scarcely noticed it.

And now in the second decade of the new century, fintech innovations seem on the cusp of transforming banking and payments systems and perhaps going on to change the nature of money and with it our understanding of safe assets.

This comes after years of loose monetary policy, low interest rates and seemingly expensive stock markets. In combination with ready access to the new trading platforms and financial sector innovation, we are facing a situation that, in all likelihood, makes sudden financial crises more likely. All investors have been challenged by cautious investments that offered little secure income and the prospect of losses in value when interest rates and inflation rose. In our opinion, these are compelling reasons to keep investments simple and not get carried away by the prospect of making easy money. There is, we believe, simply no such thing.

The aim of our book is to help investors navigate this new world. As markets are transformed, investors need to be able to think beyond dodgy online chatter and to challenge investment company salesmen who will be motivated to recommend the latest new financial product.

Instead, we offer 18 key principles that will help investors make sensible decisions when they feel tempted that they "ought to be able to do better". For example, our first chapter is called "Where's the beef?", a reminder to us all that we should only make an investment if we find the investment case convincing. The investment principles that underpin the book will help investors reduce the chance of making major investment mistakes. They are:

1. Always look for the substance in any investment proposal (Chapter 1)

2. When investing, take time to decide, then do it (Chapter 2)

3. The glory of compounding accrues most easily to those who adopt a sensible strategy and add regular contributions to it over long periods (Chapter 3)

4. Expensive fees are a dead weight that drag down living standards in retirement (Chapter 3)

5. If you see easy money to be made in the stock market or anywhere else, you have not looked hard enough (Chapter 4)

6. Star managers don't walk on water (Chapter 4)

7. Most stocks underperform the stock market (Chapter 4)

8. Be modest in your expectations for investment returns, and over time compounding will look after you (Chapter 4)

9. When investing for the long term, it is better to be a tortoise than a hare (Chapters 1, 4 and 5)

10. We don't believe anyone knows where interest rates and inflation will be in 15 years' time, and this matters (Chapter 5)

11. You will not be able to avoid the surprising bad times in the years ahead so you should know how you and your savings will cope with them (Chapter 5)

12. Investing in a global equity tracker fund can be a surprisingly sensible way to invest in equities (Chapters 6 and 8)

13. If adjusting your investments to reflect environmental, social and governance priorities, remember to keep your investments well diversified (Chapter 8)

14. In times of acute crisis, government bonds are still the investor's best friend. But over time, they are always vulnerable to inflation (Chapters 4, 5 and 9)

15. In bad times, corporate bonds always show their intrinsic and unhelpful link to stock market volatility (Chapter 9)

16. Property is at the heart of everyone's finances and well-being

17. Patient individual investors in real estate investment trusts can be in a stronger position than many institutional investors to benefit from investing in real estate (Chapter 11)

18. Investing in things you enjoy owning or supporting gives you more than just monetary rewards (Chapters 8 and 12).

Look out for these principles throughout the book.

Investment controversies

There are many popular investment books, but few provide a dispassionate up-to-date review of the controversies that surround the management of personal savings and wealth in the 21st century. How safe are government bonds and could crypto assets (and especially that subset of crypto assets called **stable coins**) provide an attractive alternative? How should the threat of man-made climate change affect investing? Is **index investing** (buying an index fund that looks to replicate the performance of a chosen stock or bond market, also known as passive investing) compatible with good governance? How much do we know about future inflation and interest rates? Is a global approach to investing best or should we have more in our home markets? These are some of the controversies that are explored in this book.

There is no need for investors to reconcile competing arguments, or to align strongly with either side of a dispute; instead, they need to think through how unresolved debate influences the uncertainty that accompanies their investment strategy. That is what this book seeks to do, in a way that is intended to be of practical use.

No investor, however large or small their wealth, needs to feel bamboozled by advisers into adopting a complicated strategy they do not understand. The book does discuss more sophisticated ways of investing, but any investor can always sit back and say, "No, I want to keep things simple but appropriate."

There is always a suitable strategy for any investor that simply combines cash, well-diversified equities and government bonds. Investment managers will almost always recommend a more expensive and more complicated strategy and they often suggest that diversification now requires an allocation away from the stock and bond markets to private markets. Private markets carry high fees, are less transparent than they sound, less flexible and normally require longer-term commitment. The arguments in favour of private market investing are less persuasive than they sound. Our book gives investors the knowledge and vocabulary they need to understand and, if necessary, challenge strategies that complicate how their money is invested.

Despite the revolution in online trading platforms, financial markets should be seen as a place to protect and grow wealth. But it is not a reliable place to grow wealthy. It is an environment in which the patience of the tortoise can compound investment returns on regular generous pension contributions into a decent pension or savings pot. The skittishness of the hare, however, is most likely to end in disappointment. Most who try their luck as full-time day traders soon conclude that it is not a sustainable career choice.

Some basic investment terms

The world of investment is full of terminology that can feel intimidating for personal investors. Here's an explanation of the some of the most common terms that will appear throughout the book. The glossary at the back of the book provides another reference, with the terms explained there shown in bold in the text on first mention.

Equities, also known as **shares** or **stocks**, represent part ownership in a company.

Fixed income or **bonds** are investments that have a predetermined schedule of interest payments (also called fixed-interest coupons) and a fixed redemption value at maturity. They represent lending to governments and companies. Creditworthy governments are expected to honour the payment terms of their debt, so government debt such as US **Treasury bonds** bear minimal credit risk and are described as "safe harbour" investments. Companies may, and sometimes do, fail to meet their payment obligations and so corporate bonds are considered to be risk assets. A **credit portfolio** is a portfolio that gives exposure to corporate and other bonds.

Cash represents investments that could earn interest as bank deposits, holdings in money market funds or in shorter maturity government issued paper (such as **Treasury bills**). **Money market funds** are professionally managed funds that invest in cash and lower risk cash-like investments.

Safe-harbour assets are expected to provide shelter against a storm and can include cash and government bonds. The protections against different risks (including loss of capital and exposure to inflation) provided by different types of government debt are discussed in Chapter 4.

Risk assets are exposed to various underlying risks and include equities, corporate bonds (and portfolios exposed to credit risk), and real estate.

Public investments are usually **listed** or **quoted** investments for which prices are regularly quoted on a formal stock exchange at which, or close to which, transactions can be completed.

Private markets refer to unlisted or unquoted investments for which price quotations are generally not readily available.

Leverage is an indication of the extent to which an investment, and thus its performance and risk, is geared or multiplied through the level of debt embedded in it.

Short selling arises when investors sell an investment that they do not own, either through selling futures or borrowing it (by providing collateral to the stock lender). In contrast, a long position is an investment that is owned.

Financial derivatives are investment contracts that are designed to replicate risk and return of direct investment in, for example, the stock markets, bond markets or foreign exchange markets.

Multi-asset funds are investment vehicles that invest across multiple types of investments, strategies and fund managers.

Hedge funds are best understood as private entrepreneurial investment companies that operate with few constraints using their own research to identify opportunities to target high returns.

Investment managers work at firms that provide investment management services. **Consultants** and **advisers** are professionals who assist investors on a broad range of financial and investment issues ranging from individual pensions, financial planning to selecting investment managers.

Road map of the book

The book unfolds over twelve chapters.

Chapter 1: Where's the beef?

We begin by emphasising the importance of seeking out the substance behind any investment proposal. Investing has become much less expensive and much more accessible so far this century. The covid-19 pandemic provides a perfect illustration of the difference between uncertainty (which we cannot measure) and risk (which we can try to measure). It's a reminder that the most common measure of investment risk – the **volatility** of investment value – is only ever a partial measure.

We also discuss the importance of financial literacy as a safeguard against fraud and betrayal and the different indicators of risk tolerance (used by advisers) and risk aversion (used by economists). The risks that matter for an investor often cannot be measured and those that might be measured often are not. The key question is, "How much risk can you tolerate?"

Chapter 2: Know thyself: can I trust my own advice or do I need an adviser?

Do investors need advisers? Investors can often be their own worst enemy when they take decisions on their own; even self-confident investors can benefit from the much broader financial planning advice from a compatible adviser. A reasonable financial plan for the future in 2022 should seem disappointingly modest compared with past market experience. We emphasise the importance for both the investor and adviser to feel that the fee rate is commensurate with the service provided.

We also explore how economics says investors ought to invest and behavioural finance's explanation of how investors invest in practice. We contrast investor preferences (which should be respected) with investor biases (which frequently lead to investment mistakes). In so doing we discuss how behaviour can help and hinder people as they invest their savings.

Chapter 3: The personal pension challenge

A defining feature of the new world of individual investing is the personal pension fed by automatic payroll deductions. We illustrate the pernicious impact on living standards of even modest inflation during retirement. We encourage those nearing retirement to explore options to delay and so increase entitlement to inflation-linked state pensions and social security. Often, this will be the most competitively priced old age insurance available. We also discuss the likelihood of incurring substantial care costs in old age and different approaches to drawing down a pension pot.

Chapter 4: What drives performance?

One of the features of personal investment during the pandemic was "herding" towards specific stocks and, at least for a time, driving their performance. We put this in the context of the returns to be expected over time from stock markets. We suggest that it is normally better to go with a less exciting, well-diversified off-the-shelf investment strategy. Counter-intuitively, new research shows that any typical stock is likely to perform worse than the market, because the exceptional performance of a very few lifts the whole market with them.

Chapter 5: Inflation, interest rates, booms and busts: is anything safe?

Many have opinions, but no one knows where interest rates and inflation will be in the decades ahead. This matters for investors.

One consequence is that the fair value of government bonds is questioned and with it the fair value for the stock market. This is just the type of environment to encourage many to look for secure premium returns. These do not exist. We discuss whether other forms of diversification and would-be safe harbours for an investor's wealth, including gold and cryptocurrencies, are useful alternatives to government bonds. In our view, they are not, but extreme political conditions might justify such investment decisions. Nevertheless, we readily recognise that the growth of cryptocurrencies and its associated block-chain record of transactions are likely to lead to an epoch-defining change in banking and in how wealth is kept secure and verified.

We also look at the recurring pattern for stock and credit markets to alternate between extended periods of deceptive calm, lasting years, and dangerous shorter episodes of manic disruption.

Chapter 6: Will model allocations help me invest better?

We suggest that a simple model allocation – or benchmark – for dividing assets between equities, bonds and cash makes sense for investors. Model allocations are used by investors large and small all around the world. The most aggregated allocations impose discipline on investment decision-making and risk-taking, even though the volatility in markets, and thus the risk of loss in investor strategies, can still fluctuate alarmingly.

We also look at how models say investors *should* invest and show summary data for how they actually *do* invest.

Chapter 7: Liquidity risk: in bad times, cash is king

An inability to turn investments into cash quickly without incurring a significant loss is known as illiquidity. This has been described as the most dangerous and least understood financial risk. Ironically, it encourages two notable heresies. One is that investors can take comfort from the reported low volatility of infrequently traded investments. The other is that if an investment is illiquid, it will offer a premium rate of return to compensate for its inflexibility. Both are misplaced.

The next four chapters examine the place of risk assets in an investor's strategy.

Chapter 8: Risk assets: global equity markets

There are currently two defining trends for equity investing. One is the enormous rise in index matching or tracking equity strategies. The other is the rise to prominence of environmental, social and governance issues.

We look at different styles of investing in stock markets, and in particular how much to invest abroad, and whether international investments should be **hedged** to manage currency risk. We conclude that an **unhedged** global approach to investing is usually the practical best approach for individual investors, as equities are risky whether or not they are hedged. However, there are exceptions and there are arguments for some home-country bias in allocating investments.

Chapter 9: Risk assets: global credit

We look at the role of corporate bonds and other types of debt. We explain how the pricing of these credit portfolios varies with stock market volatility, which is why they are properly considered to be risk assets. In times of crisis, government bonds are still the investor's best friend.

Chapter 10: Multi-asset funds and alternative investments

Multi-asset funds can be one-stop shops to meet all an investor's needs. They include simple combinations of index funds of equities, bonds and cash. More often they provide access to a wide variety of alternative investments which are not otherwise available to most individual investors. At their best, actively managed multi-asset funds have industry-leading risk management, using leverage and short selling to optimise their chances of outperforming while managing the scope for underperformance. More complex funds usually come with a much higher burden of fees than their keep-it-simple index fund competitors. But they can give access to streams of revenue and risk not otherwise easily accessed by private investors.

Chapter 11: Home ownership and real estate

Everyone needs a home, and for many the wealth committed to their house is their most valuable investment. Housing is different because it meets the need for shelter and so can be low risk, even if its price is volatile. There is often an emotional attachment to housing which echoes the appeal of art and other treasured possessions.

Investing in commercial real estate is different. This is a market that has been upended by the covid-19 pandemic. Personal investors usually invest through real estate investment trusts. They enable investors to gain the advantages of real estate investing more flexibly than institutional investors, such as pension funds and insurance companies, who directly own buildings. In the UK, traditional property funds which rely on less volatile surveyors' valuations are a less efficient way for individuals to invest in commercial property.

Chapter 12: Art and investments of passion

Plenty of people have collections of paintings, or treasured possessions items such as stamps, rare books, watches or classic cars, on which they have expended significant amounts of money. The prospect of earning an emotional, not financial, dividend from owning a beautiful work of art is invariably the catalyst for a decision to buy. This is just as well. Others have noted soberly that almost all paintings that are bought will eventually be thrown away.

Technology has transformed the making, buying and recording of ownership of much art this century. This has made the markets for fine art and treasured possessions much more efficient. We discuss how art prices appear positively correlated with income inequality and wealth.

*

If there is one overriding message we want readers of this book to absorb and reflect upon, it is the importance of always asking of any investment proposal, "Where's the beef?" Allied to this is the message that if something has gone up in price and many are buying it, that alone does not make it a worthwhile investment.

Peter Stanyer, Masood Javaid, Stephen Satchell
October 2022

1

Where's the beef?

Always look for the substance in any investment proposal

Isaac Newton, widely recognised as one of the greatest mathematicians and physicists of all time (and "presumably rational"), should have trusted his first answer to the question in this chapter heading. Instead, his greed got the better of him in the get-rich-quick speculation of his time, now known as the South Sea Bubble. Having already made a substantial profit in the early months of this early 18th-century mania, he risked three times as much, at the top of the market, and lost it all.

In the 17th century, the apocryphal speculative buyers of Dutch tulips probably saw a beautiful answer to a question that runs repeatedly throughout this book: why do you think you are making a worthwhile investment? Crypto investors should keep asking it too. Without asking that question, investors in funds that fed the enormous fraud of Bernie Madoff didn't stand a chance, whereas those who did ask, not seeing a convincing answer, steered clear.

Financial excess has repeatedly generated periods of widespread frenzied attention, as individuals think they have found a shortcut to get rich. But frenetic activity in a well-hyped, fashionable investment opportunity does not, by itself, justify involvement by more thoughtful individual investors.

Modern investing

The development of online trading and wealth management platforms this century has made easy-to-access investment accounts widely available at impressively low cost. With interest rates close to zero for years, previously solid income from bank accounts became a distant memory of older investors. A combination of easy money, financial liberalisation and, thanks to technology, unprecedented declines in transaction costs, has provided a fertile environment for innovation and, seemingly, bubbles and speculation.

These changes have also paved the way to low-cost investment strategies for modest regular savings. It is a safe bet that many large institutional funds with billions to invest struggle to perform as well as the simple index tracking strategies that are now available to individual investors with a few hundred dollars, euros or pounds to invest each month. An individual with modest savings may be unable to access sophisticated but expensive investment opportunities favoured by institutions, but despite their seemingly meagre funds, they are no longer at a clear performance disadvantage.

As we've seen, the US stock trading platform Robinhood has been the poster child for this new era of open access investing. Pioneering a now widespread US business model with no commissions, no minimum account size and a user-friendly website, individual investors seized the easy opportunity to trade. From its start in 2013, Robinhood had attracted 2 million customers by 2017 and 18 million by 2021.

At times there appeared to be a frenzy of stock trading, with internet chat rooms and message boards providing a breeding ground for market gossip and share tipping, helped in 2020 by the receipt of the $1,200 covid economic stimulus cheques sent to US citizens.

This is a different world from the late 20th century when buying an equity or an investment fund for the first time was expensive and time-consuming and frequently involved sending letters and application forms by post. That was a time when most large employers in the United States and the UK enrolled their employees in pension plans in which entitlements automatically grew with length of service and level of earnings. That world has disappeared.

Objectives, risk and uncertainty

In this new world, investors' objectives are much the same as they have always been. People save to fund expenditure in the future. This might be for their retirement, or to fund a deposit on a house purchase, a holiday, a wedding or a child's education. Or it might be to build up reserves for an unexpected rainy day, or any other purpose. In doing this, we always confront a myriad of risks and uncertainties.

The most important risks threaten the achievement of our goals. We might, for example, harness time and the prospect of superior but risky returns from patient investing. Time certainly allows superior performance to compound, but at the risk of falling increasingly short of objectives. In practice, the volatility of investments (that is, the annualised **standard deviation** of monthly investment returns) is used as a proxy for risk in investment discussions. This is often a useful indicator and is used as a guide to the likely extent of disappointing returns. It can, however, be misleading.

Often, the volatility of past investment returns is the only readily available data, but it's crucial to know how and when to qualify their use. A low number for volatility can in some predictable circumstances sugarcoat risk by suggesting, incorrectly, a low risk of extreme negative returns. We'll return to this in Chapter 4, where an illustration of this is given, though the issue is widespread and is discussed throughout the book.

To complicate matters, there is an important distinction between risk and uncertainty. Gambling on tossing a fair coin constitutes risk as the outcomes and their probabilities are fully known, even though the actual result of the coin toss is not. Being hit by meteorites, abducted by aliens and other such phenomena are different as we cannot fully describe the outcomes or their probabilities. The covid-19 pandemic reminds us that there are plenty of uncertainties that we know exist, but we cannot currently hope to model: yesterday's uncertainties are tomorrow's risks.

Risk and uncertainty: the covid-19 pandemic

The covid-19 pandemic struck out of the blue – or did it? After SARS, HIV-AIDS and swine flu, humanity did not need reminding that epidemics of deadly disease are a known threat to society and have been since the dawn of time. Experts knew this but they would not have been able to say how likely a pandemic was or when it might hit. It was a known unknown, a bad event that might strike. In the event, the adverse economic impact from covid-19 for most arose from government policy reactions to the pandemic, and especially the restrictions on social mixing and the business lockdowns, and not from its direct health consequences. This was an occasion when the benefits of holding rainy day reserves in cash proved valuable, not necessarily for seeing right through the pandemic, but at least for buying some extra time (see Chapter 6). It was also an occasion when in most countries, the government stepped in as insurer of last resort, at huge costs to their national debts. Some have suggested that the risk of further pandemics and climate change means that governments should prepare to be insurers of last resort more often in the decades ahead. This would have major implications for government debt, interest rates and perhaps inflation during the remainder of this century (see Chapter 5).

In the past, risk managers have sometimes described extreme market developments as one-in-a-million-year events, as if they could not reasonably have managed that risk because whatever happened was so unlikely to have happened. More likely, they should have known in advance that their risk model was incomplete, even if it used all the available data. Risk can be measured; uncertainty cannot.

A separate issue is the need to distinguish between threats to future income, which is a concern to a pensioner or someone saving for a pension, and threats to the value of investments, which matter more to a short-term investor who may need to have resources readily available. The volatility of investment returns and the short-term risk of losing money are relevant for the short-term investor but potentially misleading for pension savings (see Chapter 3) and inadequate as a general measure of risk. Being cautious means different things to different investors and this highlights the importance of questions being framed appropriately by advisers.

The pattern of investment returns through time matters to investors, and their perception of the risk of a bad outcome will be increased by disappointments along the way, not just the final return at some date in the future. Investors naturally revise their expectations and understanding of risk as time evolves and as their own experience (and everyone else's) grows. This focus on the risk of suffering unacceptable losses at any stage before the investor's target date (for example, when they hope to retire) has highlighted the dangers of mismeasuring risk (see Chapter 6).

Risk is about bad outcomes, and a bad outcome that might arrive at a bad time is especially damaging and requires particularly attractive rewards to compensate for facing that risk. As discussed, investment advisers typically judge the riskiness of an investment by its volatility, but in the words of Antti Ilmanen not all volatilities are equal, and the timing of bad outcomes matters for risk as much as the scale of those bad outcomes.[1]

A theme throughout this book is that personal investors should think about how investments might perform in bad times as the key to understanding how much risk they are taking. There is little discussion of what constitutes a bad time, which will vary from investor to investor, but it is best captured by Ilmanen, who defines it as a time when an extra dollar of ready cash feels especially valuable.

One way to help manage the risk of being wrong-footed by bad times is to reflect on risk-taking during the good times, when inappropriate risk-taking often gets rewarded, not called out. This theme is captured by a photograph at the front of Frank Sortino and Stephen Satchell's book *Managing Downside Risk in Financial Markets*. It shows Karen Sortino on safari in Africa, petting an intimidating rhino. The caption reads, "Just because you got away with it, doesn't mean you didn't take any risk."

As we'll see in Chapter 4, this may be a matter of being seduced by a seemingly exceptional manager performance which may hide embedded risk of exceptional negative returns. In any event, there is an increasingly recognised need for financial education. This is reflected in the number of universities and schools that run courses for their students to prepare them for looking after their financial well-being. The rise of self-investing and personal responsibility for pension provision puts a premium on financial literacy.

Financial literacy: well worth the effort

Individuals who do not have basic numeracy and financial literacy skills can easily be disadvantaged in this new environment of flexible working, portable pension pots and online trading. This is a significant issue because around the world tens of millions have become investors. In recent years international survey evidence has consistently found high levels of financial illiteracy.

This is shown by a poor understanding of three core financial concepts:

1. the compounding of interest payments
2. the impact of inflation
3. the benefits of risk diversification.

Any investor needs some understanding of these, and they are also especially important for this book and our core investment principles. The recognition of their importance has led to a growing focus on financial literacy and investment principles among schoolchildren and the publication of age-appropriate books to address these challenges early on.[2]

Financial literacy is different from numeracy. Being numerate does not ensure that you are financially literate, or that you have an intuitive feel for the important difference between risk (which can be measured) and uncertainty (which cannot).

Company-sponsored defined-contribution retirement funds, such as 401(k) plans in the United States, typically reduce the burden of decision-making imposed on employees by having default funds into which the overwhelming majority of employee contributions flow. Default plans outsource decision-making for retirement saving to simple structures designed by investment professionals.

Increasingly these default funds are target date funds, where the sole decision needed from the contributor is their expected retirement date (but see Chapter 3). Contributors should seek reassurance about whether the default contribution rates are likely to support their hoped-for standard of living in retirement; it is most likely they will need to contribute more each month. Given the target retirement date, the default strategy is designed to evolve automatically over the years as recommended by the company's advisers.

Default funds may nudge employees towards better patterns of retirement saving, but financial literacy is still needed to avoid pitfalls in financial management. One finding from research, which may have worrying implications for the future, is the poor appreciation of the impact of even modest inflation on the standard of living (see Chapter 3). This seems to be a particular issue in countries that have had little recent experience of rising prices. The importance of allowing for the impact of inflation on living standards has been highlighted by much higher worldwide inflation in the early 2020s.

Other aspects of financial illiteracy include a widespread failure to understand investment concepts (such as **stocks** and bonds) that are routinely used by financial advisers. Research has also shown that education is not necessarily a good proxy for financial literacy, and that women are on average less financially confident and less financially literate than men.

Conversely, individuals with better financial literacy were more likely to plan for retirement, better able to withstand unexpected financial shocks, and to feel more financially secure. Investing in financial literacy may lead to better financial outcomes and educational courses have been shown to lead to higher levels of regular pension contributions.

Another strategy for investors who readily admit to finding financial concepts challenging is to err towards professionally designed simple investment strategies, which are easier to understand.

Fraud and betrayal

At the end of November 2008, the accounts of the clients of Bernard L. Madoff Investment Securities LLC, an investment adviser registered by the US Securities and Exchange Commission (SEC), had a supposed aggregate value of $64.8 billion invested in the allegedly sophisticated investment strategy run by Bernie Madoff. But it was a fraud. His deception had started sometime in the 1970s. It lasted until December 11th 2008 when he was arrested and his business was exposed as a huge scam, probably the largest securities fraud the world has ever known.

The amounts that Madoff's investors thought they owned were inflated by fictitious investment performance. The amount that Madoff actually controlled was further reduced because early investors, who then withdrew money, were paid their inflated investment values with billions of dollars provided by later investors. The court-appointed liquidator has estimated the actual losses to investors of money they originally invested to be around $17.5 billion.

Nevertheless, at one stage, investors believed that they had assets – which, unknown to them, were mostly fictitious – worth almost four times as much. By June 2022, the liquidators had recovered or entered into agreements to recover, often from early beneficiaries of the fraud, $14.5 billion or about 83% of the estimated losses of amounts originally invested with the firm. Although the trustee for the liquidation has recovered much more than was initially feared, distributions to investors represent only 21% of the aggregate inflated value reported by Madoff before it collapsed. Investors have been left nursing huge losses from what they had believed was their wealth.

If risk is about bad outcomes, to be a victim of fraud is a particularly bad outcome. But when investors look after their own savings and investments, they are often their own worst enemies. Many people expect savings and investments, in which they have no particular fascination, to be a difficult subject that they do not expect to understand. They are often tempted to take a shortcut and, in the words of Daniel Kahneman, a Nobel laureate in economics, "think fast", which can lead to avoidable mistakes, rather than "thinking slow", which requires some concentration and effort.

Our lazy inclination to think fast is readily exploited by fraudsters who are attracted to our money and to our behavioural weaknesses like bees to a honey pot. The enormous Madoff fraud provides salutary lessons for both individual and professional investors. It is a mistake to think "it couldn't happen to me". It could, and do-it-yourself investors are probably particularly vulnerable. Professional advisers who expect to be able to find outperforming investment managers (see Chapter 2) are also susceptible to being misled. Fraud in financial markets is depressingly common.

Bernie Madoff's investment strategy seemingly offered the attractive combination of a long-run performance comparable to the stock market but with little volatility, supposedly thanks to clever use of financial **derivatives**, such as **options**, which were said by Madoff and his often-unwitting sales teams cleverly to provide insurance against stock market setbacks, while benefiting from market appreciation.

Marketing material from fund distributors presented the track record of Madoff's fraud showing the seductive combination of apparently low risk and high, but perhaps not outrageous, returns. But an experienced adviser or investor should immediately recognise that Madoff's track record looked odd. It is always safe to assume that there are no low-risk routes to returns well above the return on cash.

Madoff's strategy was a simple **Ponzi scheme**, whereby a fraudulent rate of return is promised, seemingly verified in this case by the experience of those early investors who had been able to withdraw inflated amounts. So long as only a few investors demand their money back, they can be paid what they have been told their investment is now worth. But what they had been told was a lie, and the inflated returns were delivered to a few by redirecting cash from the most recent investors. As with any Ponzi scheme, Madoff relied on robbing Peter to pay Paul.

These scams always collapse as soon as the demands of investors who want to sell their investments outweigh the cash provided by new investors. The Madoff fraud grew so large because it survived many years. Its undoing was the credit squeeze of 2008 when too many investors, who were presumably happy with Madoff's reported investment performance, had to withdraw funds to meet losses elsewhere. This caused the Madoff house of cards to collapse.

The victims were mostly based in the United States, but there were also many from around the world. Many were introduced to his fund through personal, investment adviser or wealth manager recommendations. These would have stressed his respectable community and business pedigree as a former chairman of the NASDAQ stock exchange and philanthropist.

Madoff's investors included wealthy individuals, charities, some wealth managers but, interestingly, relatively few institutional investors. Their analysts were unable to find a plausible explanation for Madoff's apparent excellent performance. It is safe to say that this was not because they identified it as fraudulent but because they could not understand it.

A large part of the problem of fraud is that it's easy for people to be seduced by the belief that they have found a low-risk way of performing surprisingly well. And yet, surprisingly good investment performance *always* involves risk.

Madoff was not an isolated example of large-scale fraud or suspected fraud, even though its scale was unprecedented.

These episodes provide important lessons for investors and for their advisers. Some of Madoff's investors were following the recommendations of investment advisers, who appeared to take pride in their professional diligence in identifying outperforming investment managers. The advisers could then often point to the name of one of the leading accountancy firms as the auditor of the third-party feeder fund that was the conduit to Madoff Investment Securities. However, this provided no protection for the investors themselves.

How was someone who had followed the recommendation of an adviser or a friend supposed to identify the risks? Ten old lessons emerge.

1. The old and seemingly trivial saying that "if it looks too good to be true, it probably is" remains one of the most valuable pieces of investment advice anyone can give.

2. Returns in excess of the return offered by the government can be achieved only by taking risk.

3. Risk is most obvious when an investment is volatile and is least obvious when a risky investment has not yet shown much volatility. This is rarely mentioned in books on investment.

4. Investors should question an adviser who recommends a low volatility investment that offers superior returns.

5. Do not invest in something you do not understand simply because a group of your peers is doing so. A desire to conform can explain many decisions that you would otherwise not take.

6. Whatever your adviser says, make sure that your investments are well diversified. But keep in mind that diversification is most difficult to assess when risky investments are not obviously volatile.

7. Pay particular attention if an adviser gives you inconvenient cautious advice, such as a recommendation to avoid something

that you would like to invest in or advice to sell a hitherto well performing investment.

8. Social status may not be a good indicator of honesty.

9. Do not assume that because an investment firm is regulated that the regulators have been able to check that everything is all right.

10. The ability to rely on good due diligence by investment managers is the key to minimising exposure to risk of fraud. An authoritative post-mortem report on the Madoff affair is called "Madoff: A Riot of Red Flags". Most private investors would not spot these red flags, but it was not by chance that only a few institutional investors lost money with Madoff. A challenge for private investors is to ensure that they also have access to good-quality manager due diligence.

How much risk can you tolerate?

How much risk you're prepared to take is fundamental to any investment strategy. Bear in mind that academics and advisers approach it in different ways.

Academic economists use mathematical assumptions to model risk aversion. This measures the extra compensation an investor requires to accept more risk. This may change as circumstances (such as wealth) change. Such assumptions are attractive in part because they can be used in models but also because they can be estimated empirically.

In contrast, behavioural finance stresses the importance of the asymmetry of response between gains and losses. Rather than risk aversion, this is known as "loss aversion" (see Chapter 2).

Wealth managers have traditionally used questionnaires to categorise client attitudes to risk-taking. These questionnaires may cover investors' circumstances (age, family, income, wealth, expenditure plans and so on) as well as their attitude to risk. One problem is that questions posed by wealth managers about risk may use language and concepts that are unfamiliar to non-experts.

In recent years, psychometric profiling services, typically developed with academic researchers, have become widely used by wealth managers to assess and compare attitudes to risk. This has led to a step change in the rigour of profiling. It has been accelerated by the rise of largely automated online investment services provided by so-called robo-advisers.

These services need to assess the suitability of their clients for different investment products with little direct interaction with those clients before the adviser recommends an investment. The robo-adviser needs to be satisfied that suitable investment advice is being given to the investor. One inconvenience, though, can be that clients often give inconsistent answers to related but different questions. This often calls for human intervention (rather than a machine-driven response) to iron out apparent discrepancies. In addition, robo-advisers may subsequently introduce human advisers to promote new products.[3]

The responses to one large international risk-profiling service shows some interesting patterns. The pattern of responses does not vary much by country: individuals' tolerance for risk is, on average, fairly stable over time; women tend to be more cautious than men (which is important for investing family wealth); and investment professionals tend to be more tolerant of risk than their clients (who in turn tend to be marginally more tolerant of risk than the population as a whole).

But the data do show a wide variation of responses for individuals around these average characteristics. This can matter if advisers use typical responses to make assumptions about the attitudes to risk-taking of individual investors.

It seems likely that well-designed psychometric testing helps to categorise the risk appetite of investors better than ad hoc questionnaires. It also seems that cautious people probably cannot be educated out of their disposition to be cautious. However, a single score on a risk-tolerance questionnaire, even a well-designed one, will not be an adequate guide to an investor's willingness or capacity to take risk.

Discussions of risk-taking need to reflect threats to the security of future income as much, if not more than, threats to future value of investments. The two are not the same, and in Chapter 4 we discuss how a government bond which may provide a stable income for many years will at the same time have a value that fluctuates as interest rates change.

Investors will sometimes hear advisers talk of the need to take a particular level of risk in order to meet their objectives. This may be contrasted with the investor's wish to take risk (sometimes called risk appetite) or, which may not be the same thing, ability to take risk (sometimes known as risk capacity). Investors should challenge such talk by asking if the adviser is saying that their apparently reasonable objectives are on reflection, not reasonable, but are beyond their prudent reach. This is explored further in the next chapter, which looks at how an adviser can help align people's finances with realistic objectives.

2

Know thyself: can I trust my own advice or do I need an adviser?

When investing, we can be our own worst enemies. A compatible adviser can help protect us from ourselves

Many investors feel, rightly or wrongly, that they do not need an investment adviser. At the start of an investor's journey, investing a regular savings contribution, we would recommend that the investor reflects on the 18 investment principles listed in the Introduction to this book. If, however, the investor starts by investing a life-changing sum, for example an inheritance or a retirement lump sum, we would recommend that, in addition to reflecting on our investment principles, they take time to think through reasons for seeking or not seeking advice.

One reason for seeking advice is the realisation that the advice that they might need is broader than investment advice. Even confident self-advised private investors should consider whether they need financial planning advice. Financial planning is much broader. It includes discussions about planning for retirement (however distant that might be), how much young investors should save, how best to secure a stable income, provision for old age care and for any dependants, and then issues around inheritance planning. There is also tax advice, an area in which even investment experts are not necessarily competent.

When investors reflect on these broader issues, important

aspects of risk-taking may surface. Frequently these discussions reveal differing attitudes to risk-taking within a family. Investment advice is only part of this. When investors follow investment advice, they need to check that the investment arrangement is appropriately diversified. The danger over long periods of time is that they will pay high fees for an arrangement of expensive equity and bond managers, whose combined performance and risk approximates to that of an expensive index fund.

If an investor is sure that they do not need an investment adviser, it still makes sense to agree a fee rate for an occasional financial planning and investment "health check". The hourly rate might seem high, but this is partly because of the regulatory cost of due diligence that an adviser needs to undertake to know their client.

Investors should ensure that the advisory fees they pay look sensible in relation to their wealth. When investors appoint advisers, they should make sure that they are comfortable with the overall level of fees, and they should from time to time, ask their advisers whether they would take their own advice and make a recommended investment for themselves. There is not necessarily a link between the quality of advice and the level of fees, although over periods of years, differences in fee levels can make a significant difference to wealth accumulation.

One benchmark for fees paid to an adviser could be the cost of a well-diversified strategy of index matching equities, bonds and cash strategy which is readily available direct from some investment managers. Bear in mind, though that, in isolation, these off-the-shelf strategies will miss the value and reassurance of receiving formal advice on questions of sustainable pension income, vulnerability to inflation and other risks, managing changes in personal and family circumstances, and also taxation. They also miss out the value of simple hand-holding when the going gets tough (which it will).

An adviser should also provide a readily available sounding board to challenge the latest get-rich-quick schemes which will captivate social media from time to time. Superficially such advice may come for free, but the underlying relationship provides fee income for the adviser and access to advice for the investor. The self-advised investor misses out on this.

When investors do choose to appoint an investment adviser, that appointment is likely to be among the most important investment decisions that they take. The adviser is likely to influence strongly the investment strategy that an investor adopts, and how their wealth and the income it generates, evolve over time. Good advice is valuable.

Often, the greatest value will be in the initial discussions about objectives, time horizon and risk-taking. These discussions can be intensely personal, and for the relationship to be successful, the investor needs to be frank with an adviser and there needs to be respect and trust between the two. If a simple investment structure of stocks, bonds and cash is established, the need for advice in subsequent years should involve significantly less cost.

Investment beliefs

Investment advice is often influenced by the views of the adviser. Different advisers embrace different approaches to investment which often reflect deeply held beliefs about how best to invest. An adviser's opinions about wealth and investment management need to be well aligned and suitable for meeting the objectives of the investor for the relationship to be successful.

The contrasting recommendations that different advisers make to investors will reflect their varying opinions on the costs and benefits of paying high or low fees, of accepting illiquidity, and on the ability to time markets. In brief, they will reflect an adviser's views on the advantages of different styles of investing. An important part of building trust in a relationship with an adviser is for investors to have an understanding of their adviser's investment beliefs, and to find them both credible and appropriate for their particular circumstances.

These differences of opinion are debated by the largest

institutional investors, but they are equally relevant to a modest individual investor. Institutional investors often describe their views on these debates as their "investment beliefs". These are tailored to their own circumstances, and they reflect (or should reflect) the way they invest.

A written set of investment beliefs can be a record that puts an agreed framework around discussions about new investments and understanding investment performance. An investor could ask a potential adviser whether they have written down their own set of investment beliefs (one side of paper should be adequate). This should summarise a coherent view of the opportunities offered by markets and whether the investor is well placed to exploit them.

An advantage of a concise summary, whether written or spoken, of an adviser's investment beliefs is that it can help to highlight potential red flags. For example, Chapter 4's discussion of investment returns should encourage an investor to question any assumption that a strategy will outperform in the future. This is often difficult for non-specialists to assess.

A financial plan that an investor agrees to buy will always look more reassuring if the performance that the adviser expects, or assumes, from bond and stock markets is strong. This is separate from whether the adviser expects to be able to find outperforming managers and it is a common problem with personal financial plans.

In 2022, there is a near consensus among investment strategists that investors need to adjust expectations and accept lower expected returns in the decades ahead (This is discussed extensively in Chapter 4.) Belt tightening is the overriding message.

This does not help to sell investment plans to investors. Advisers should be asked for an explanation of the return expected from the proposed strategy. The adviser should also be asked to quantify the assumed drag on performance from investment and advice fees. In 2021, leading academics went on record to say that a balanced strategy of equity and bonds can be assumed to earn only "about a third of the real return enjoyed by the previous three generations.

Many savers, investors, pension plans and institutions are challenged by the low-return world."[1]

A further risk for self-advised investors is that they may not have properly thought through their attitudes to good and bad times in investment markets. This can be particularly dangerous if they fail to account sufficiently for the likelihood of bad times in how they design their strategy. A poorly self-designed strategy, for example, might generate income in good times only by incurring risks of loss of capital and income in bad times. This could easily prove to be an irreversible mistake.

Conflicts of interest

The scope for conflicts of interest between investors and advisers has been greatly lessened in recent years, but it can be an issue in some relationships. Academics call the potential for conflicts of interest between investors and their advisers "the principal–agent problem" or, more loosely, "agency issues". These can arise because the principal (the investor) has inferior access to information than the agent (for example, the investment adviser). Such information asymmetries provide much studied areas of market failure (not just in finance), leading to adverse selection of low-quality products. These asymmetries can encourage advisers to use superior information in a way that serves their own interest more than the best interest of the investor.

One way in which investors can reduce their exposure to conflicts is to distance themselves from much of the detailed investment decision-making, and to invest in an appropriate risk-graded strategy or multi-asset fund (see Chapters 3 and 10).

Investors may still be sold what an adviser wishes to sell rather than deciding to buy what they need. The best safeguard is for investors to satisfy themselves that their interests and those of their advisers are appropriately aligned (which is often encouraged by regulation), and that conflicts of interest are in the open. In practice, reassurance on this will depend more on the characters of the individuals concerned than the institutional arrangements within which they work.

Know thyself

Investors can sometimes be their own worst enemies when they take their own advice. A compatible investment adviser can help to reduce this danger though, as discussed, the selection of the adviser itself carries risk.

In recent decades, research by experimental psychologists and advances in behavioural finance have enormously enriched economists' understanding of how we take decisions. These insights have shown that we routinely make choices in ways that differ markedly from the assumptions that underlie the traditional models of economists and finance academics. These insights matter, as they suggest that, in many instances, investors are inclined to take worse decisions than traditional finance would predict. An understanding of these weaknesses will help to improve financial decision-making.

Traditional models in finance can be caricatured in this way: "If investors are rational, and if markets function with textbook efficiency, then investors ought to behave as follows." (Later on, we look at ways in which markets are less than efficient. Here, the focus is more on how we take decisions.) Traditional investment recommendations have assumed that investors should prefer diversified to undiversified portfolios of risky investments, and that they should view the risk of losses consistently with their attitude to the opportunity for gains. It turns out that this is not how investors always behave.

That's why it's so important that investors have some understanding of the potential weaknesses of how traditional finance models assume investors behave. A simple illustration will suffice.

Many people buy lottery tickets; they expect to lose money, but they hope to gain riches. Traditional finance implicitly finds this behaviour inefficient, but it can be rational as it provides the best legal way to have at least some chance (however remote) of securing riches in the short term.[2] If you do not buy a lottery ticket, it is certain that you will not win. An understanding of our willingness to gamble in some predictable circumstances, to overpay for insurance in others, and to be reluctant to pay for insurance (such as a life **annuity**) even when self-insurance may be very risky, can help us to manage our finances better.

Research has led to strong conclusions about the intuitive biases that affect how individuals take both instinctive and even thoughtful decisions and how they form preferences. This indicates, for example, a need for investor education. But investors and their advisers should be aware of these biases since they will help determine reactions to a range of predictable market developments.

Investor biases

Psychologists have documented systematic patterns of bias in how people form views and take decisions. These are relevant for how we form investment opinions, and then how we take investment decisions. Among these are the following.

- A general characteristic of *optimism and wishful thinking*. It would be naive to think that this characteristic did not affect views on investment.
- *Overconfidence.* A tendency to put too much faith in individual intuition.
- *Confirmation bias.* A ready acceptance as proof of any information that reinforces existing views.
- *Self-attribution.* A tendency to attribute any success that we may enjoy to our own innate ability and unusual skill. Equally, self-attribution tends to attribute disappointments to bad luck rather than a lack of skill. In investment terms: profit reflects skill, losses reflect bad luck.
- This is also associated with *hindsight bias*: individuals are often sure, after the event, that they had expected whatever happened to happen: "It was obvious it was going to happen, wasn't it?"

Or, if the outcome was a bad outcome: "It was a disaster waiting to happen." Unfortunately, the future is rarely so clear.

■ By *representativeness*, or *stereotyping*, individuals are too quick to conclude that they understand developments based on too little information. For example, 100 years of stock and bond market performance history sounds like a long time, but it represents only five separate (non-overlapping) 20-year periods, which is a small sample. In these circumstances, it is safest to be cautious before drawing conclusions. Other information, such as company profits and price levels could support stronger conclusions.

■ *Conservatism*. This arises when it is widely recognised that the available data are insufficient to support strong conclusions. In this case, a common error is to place too little weight on the available evidence, or even to disregard it and to rely solely on prior expectations.

■ *Anchoring*. A bias that makes people gravitate towards a quantity that has been suggested before considering the appropriate answer. One common example is the proportion of investments that ought to be invested in the stock market. Inevitably the answer will be strongly influenced by what the investor is told the norm is. This is understandable (though often not appropriate). Anchoring is a surprisingly widespread phenomenon, and it can easily lead to an investor being misled.

■ *Belief perseverance* is when people cling to prior opinions for too long when confronted with contrary evidence. In this way, individuals demonstrate a reluctance to search for evidence that contradicts their previous views.

Biases often represent mental shortcuts (sometimes called **heuristics**), which we use to avoid having to process large quantities of information. These shortcuts may derive from an established opinion of how markets work. For example, many investors and advisers expect to be able to identify good investment managers who will outperform. They are likely to be pleased rather than sceptical when initial data suggest outperformance. Sceptics, however, are more likely to ascribe outperformance to transient luck, and may be puzzled by apparent evidence of good managers.

These differences in received wisdom can lead to those shortcuts. For example, some may think that much more analysis is needed before a decision is taken. Others may conclude readily that the appropriate course of action is self-evident. This type of shortcut will have led some to feel comfortable in the years before 2008 that they had found a good manager in fraudster Bernie Madoff.

Increasing complexity (for example of investment products) makes it more likely that decisions will rely on shortcuts because of the sheer amount of available, relevant information. The practical alternative to using shortcuts may often appear to be indecision. But where a decision appears to have relied on such a shortcut and the decision goes wrong, hindsight can be embarrassing. The adoption of a set of investment beliefs (see above) provides one tried and tested way to facilitate consistent and often faster decision-making.

Even when investors can consider potential biases dispassionately, there is no escape from the danger of regret risk. Regret is the emotion that individuals feel if they can easily imagine having acted in a way that would have led to a more favourable outcome. For investors, this leads to the common (almost universal) dilemma of how and when to implement new investment decisions, even if investment risk arguments point to the desirability of immediate implementation (see Chapter 6). Good process, probably supported by a compatible adviser, should lead to more considered (and better) decision-making. It also helps establish confidence in the existence of a steady hand at the tiller.

Investor preferences

Preferences should be distinguished from biases. If biases should be managed, preferences should be respected and reflected in investment strategy, in so far as it is both feasible and sensible.

There are two areas of investor preference that have been highlighted by behavioural finance.

The first is *loss aversion*, which has been described as the most significant contribution of psychology to behavioural economics.

The second is **mental accounting**, which reflects the way in which people typically assign sums of money to different actual or notional accounts for different purposes with varying degrees of risk tolerance, depending on the importance of achieving that objective.

Loss aversion

Loss aversion suggests that disappointing performance disproportionately undermines investor confidence or, in other words, losses loom larger than gains. Although alternative estimates differ, the accepted rule of thumb is that investment losses weigh twice as heavily as equivalent investment gains.

This asymmetry matters, if only because investment banks have mastered the art of persuading investors to buy investment products which offer a seductive combination of little fear and much hope. There are no free lunches, and over time these products should be expected to drag on investor performance while enriching bankers.

Behavioural experiments have highlighted the importance of how a question is asked or framed as a determinant of the reaction to it. The choice of an investment benchmark helps to frame expectations for performance and whether an investor should be pleased or disappointed with an investment result.

An investor, for example, may be disappointed that a fund has lagged well behind the performance of the stock market. The adviser, by contrast, may try to persuade clients to be happy that the fund has shown some growth in value. How expectations are set at the outset for an investment can become as important as the subsequent performance in determining whether an investment is judged to be successful, or even whether an investment manager is paid a bonus.

One of the differences between this approach and conventional finance theory is that the investor's attitude differs according to whether they think that they are currently doing well or badly. In traditional finance, decisions are based on final wealth. While these differences may sound academic, this behavioural research (called **prospect theory**) offers a rich set of explanations and is supported by surveys of investor behaviour.

These reveal inclinations to:

- sell winning investments after a run of good performance
- buy investments with characteristics of lottery tickets even though the most likely result by far is the loss of the cost of the lottery ticket
- hold on to loss-making investments to avoid the pain of realising losses. This offers some hope of recouping losses, at the risk of incurring even bigger ones
- buy insurance, to avoid the small risk of even some loss.

Mental accounting and behavioural portfolio theory

A division of investments between safety-first, cautious accounts to meet basic needs, and more aggressive aspirational accounts to meet less critical or simply more distant objectives is one of the predictions of the mental accounting framework of behavioural finance.

This approach is not found anywhere in the traditional finance textbooks, where the efficient management of an investor's total assets and liabilities is taken for granted. However, it is common (some would say common sense) in everyday experience. This can be seen in Chapter 3 where there is a discussion of the challenges faced by individuals in arranging their finances to fund a regular income, to maintain an emergency cash reserve and perhaps to build up additional reserves to fund potential end of life care.

Mental accounting helps financial resources to be targeted for different purposes. Some goals are critical, but others are just nice to have. Traditional finance addresses the performance and risk of the total portfolio, which would presume taking either a little or a lot more risk with all the money. However, if an overall strategy comprises a mixture of a holding of risk-free assets and an allocation to market risk, the traditional and mental accounting approaches can be the same.

This means that, in any situation, there will always be strategies that are demonstrably inefficient or that involve a clearly inappropriate risk profile. There will also be a range of strategies that are each broadly appropriate, given our current state of knowledge of the markets and an investor's attitude to risk. This can give a surprisingly wide scope for preferences to be reflected in investment strategy, while still staying consistent with the overriding desire to adhere to goals and objectives.

Some things are clear. First, it is important for investors and, where they are employed, their advisers, to benefit from the insights of behavioural finance to understand better the influences on their own decision-making and preferences. Advice and strategy can then be adapted as appropriate.

This does not provide an excuse for ignoring the fundamental principles of diversification, **correlations** between different investments or the need to tailor policies to the time horizon of investment objectives. Equally, it would be arrogant to suggest that it is always poor practice for individuals to purchase the investment equivalent of lottery tickets. This may be an efficient way of maximising the chances of acquiring riches, but it needs to be pursued in the full knowledge of its limited chances of success.

It's just one illustration of why investors need to understand how behaviour and bias will influence their own – and their advisers'

– views on investment, and the potential profits and pitfalls this brings. The cost of a good, trusting relationship with a compatible adviser might be a price worth paying to help navigate this potential minefield.

3

The personal pension challenge

The glory of compounding accrues most easily to those who adopt a sensible strategy and add regular contributions to it over long periods

Expensive fees are a dead weight that drag down living standards in retirement

This century has seen an enormous change in pension provision by employers in the United States, the UK and other countries. Old-style defined benefit pension arrangements have all but disappeared from the pension offering to new employees outside the government sector around the world. They have been replaced for private sector staff by individual investment accounts in employer-sponsored personal pension plans. This has shifted the responsibility and challenge for funding pensions from employers to employees.

Pension arrangements are now at the mercy of the personal decisions of millions in a way that was largely unknown in earlier generations. Assessing the adequacy of an individual's accumulation of savings from work to support them in old age has been described by Nobel laureate Professor William Sharpe as "the nastiest, hardest problem" he has ever come across in finance. When an individual is not a member of an employer's pension arrangement, their first task (and often the most important) is to choose a trusted adviser, but often it is far from clear how best to do this (see Chapter 2). Millions are in good company in finding this all very difficult.

Typically, sponsoring companies mitigate some of this personal responsibility by suggesting "set and forget" default model strategies into which employee contributions are commonly paid and then left to accumulate. If they are lucky, such default contributors will from the outset be nudged to have their pension savings kept as a fixed proportion of their pay, and so benefiting from any pay increases over time.

This transformation in pension arrangements leaves employees directly exposed to the impact of the behavioural biases discussed in Chapter 2, as well their failure to understand risk. More positively, they also enable savers (should they wish) to let their own circumstances and preferences influence their pension arrangements. It also exposes individual investors to the burden of funding pensions from prospective market returns, which are expected to be much less generous than in recent decades (see Chapter 4).

Individual decision-making now covers the adequacy of pension-saving, the appropriate ways to invest those savings and then, when retirement beckons, how to use those savings to fund their pension. The choices include whether to buy a regular annuity income from an insurance company and, if so, whether it should be fixed in money terms or increase over time. In practice, few draw a lifetime annuity (though it is a standard recommendation from economists). Instead, individuals focus on the rate at which to draw from the accumulated pot of retirement savings. An occasional question is whether to spend part of the retirement savings on an annuity, leaving the rest as a flexible drawdown.

As a financial adviser would readily tell an economist, financial needs in retirement do not usually follow a stable path. One consequence of increasing life expectancy is that growing numbers of younger pensioners or those approaching retirement can find themselves sandwiched between commitments to their much older parents and supporting their children. In many families, this will also include the need to make financial provision for a dependant with special needs. Adding to the worry and stress, those on the cusp of drawing their pension need to consider the possibility of living to great old age and perhaps, also, of being among the minority who incur substantial care costs in their last years.

This difficulty with organising an individual's pension income reflects the need to juggle, judge and model a tough range of variables and uncertainties over the course of their lives. This includes:

- their pension savings rate
- their existing fund of pension and other savings and investments
- their income and how it may evolve
- any continuing financial responsibilities to their family
- their customary standard of living
- their retirement dates
- the plausible range of their life expectancy
- whether they continue to work part-time while drawing a pension
- their entitlement to inflation-linked social security or state old age pension, and when best to start drawing these benefits
- the equity in their home
- the risk of incurring uninsured, substantial nursing or care home costs in old age
- how to invest and the range of returns expected from their accumulated savings
- the plausible ranges of inflation over the decades ahead
- the rate of interest and how it is expected to evolve over time
- their appetite and ability to tolerate risk and uncertainty
- their current and likely tax status
- the fees and taxes paid on accumulated savings

- whether and how each of these risks, opportunities and preferences are shared with a spouse or partner.

This range of uncertainties and required decisions suggests a need for advice across a wide range of topics. At its best, this advice will include discussion of whether these uncertainties and choices offset each other. The personal pension challenge is not primarily an investment issue, and the investment aspects of personal pensions need to be assessed alongside the non-pension savings and other resources (especially housing) of the retiree.

For many people approaching retirement, their most valuable assets are the equity stake in their homes and their accumulated retirement savings. Downsizing to a less expensive home, where this is a realistic option, provides one efficient way of improving diversification: it lessens the stake in a particular house and it frees up **liquidity** to meet financial needs. However, lifestyle also matters, and for many "there's no place like home". This suggests a psychic or emotional return to home ownership which has parallels with the rewards from owning other treasured possessions, such as a work of art (see Chapters 11 and 12).

Reverse mortgages (commonly known in the UK as equity release) provide another way of raising cash to meet the expenses of old age without disrupting the retiree's lifestyle. They enable the elderly to borrow against the security of their home. The accumulated interest due is rolled up with the loan and paid when the pensioner moves to a new house or dies. This can severely diminish the pensioner's estate if the pensioner lives to a great age. A lifetime annuity would shift longevity risk to an insurance company, but this is no free lunch. It directly places the risk of early mortality on the pensioner's estate (which will be severely diminished in the event of an early death by the cost of the annuity).

The best choices are made following informed discussion with an adviser, taking account of the terms being offered, and the aversion of the investor to the risk of losses and missed opportunities.

Financial markets can provide insurance against some of these risks. Consciously or otherwise, each individual has to decide which risks to insure and how to avoid overspending on insurance. Confronted with so much information to process and so many different decisions to take, the instinct is to take readily available mental shortcuts (see Chapter 2). These shortcuts will reflect a range of prior beliefs, which are unlikely to capture efficiently the trade-offs that preferably should be made when designing a suitable financial plan for retirement.

Retirement date uncertainty

Some of these uncertainties can also be valuable sources of flexibility. Date of retirement is one; another is part-time work after leaving mainstream work. The ability to continue working and to delay drawing a pension is the easiest way for many to enhance their retirement income. This gives a valuable option for those with borderline sufficient retirement savings who are able to exploit such opportunities. This is especially valuable in a two-income home.

For others though, these options are not available, and anyone's prospective retirement date is a further source of uncertainty. Often this is not for the individual to choose. A 2014 report from Merrill Lynch and the consultancy Age Wave found that 55% of US pensioners surveyed retired earlier than planned. Three-quarters of these early retirements were involuntary, explained by personal health problems, unemployment or the need to care for a family member.

The Just Group published a survey in late 2019 of retired and semi-retired men and women in the UK over the age of 55, which gave similar results. It found that two-thirds of respondents had retired earlier than planned for the same groups of reasons (ill health, unemployment or the need to care for a dependent). These results show that although we may target a particular retirement date, it often proves not to be ours to choose.

This theme is explored in a 2020 academic article on early retirement risk.[1] Uncertainty about date of retirement, the authors say, is often "not a buffer against shocks but rather a shock itself". Examining US annual surveys of the elderly from 1998 to 2012 they found that just over a quarter of US retirements were involuntary and that once forced retirement occurs, significant financial losses often follow.

According to the research, unexpected early retirement commonly involves the loss of several years of earnings. It also tends to increase following a sustained downturn in the stock market. For example, 46% of retirements in the United States in 2009 (that is, immediately after the global financial crisis) were involuntary. Overall, forced early retirement risk is highly correlated with the stock market. (However, during the covid-19 pandemic, the stock market was notably robust and large numbers of employees seem to have retired earlier than expected for a range of reasons.)

The research concluded that in the years before retirement, employment income changes from being a bond-like source of dependable income into a much more risky and uncertain resource. Forced retirement risk, therefore, crowds out stock market investments in the optimal retirement plan in the years before intended retirement.

How long might my retirement last?

Individuals commonly underestimate the typical length of retirement. They also underestimate the likelihood of living longer than average, to great old age.

According to the Stanford Center on Longevity, two in three American men and half of women of pre-retirement age underestimate the life expectancy of a 65-year-old. A corresponding survey in 2018 in the UK by Just Group found that adults aged between 40 and 54 underestimate their life expectancy by around ten years. This pessimism leads to a reduced focus on the possibility of living longer than average, and the increased expense that it entails. Actual experience is reflected in Table 3.1, which shows that over the last 40 years there has been a doubling of the proportion of

TABLE 3.1 **Twice as many elderly live beyond age 84 now than 40 years ago**
Percentage of all deaths by age in 1979 and 2019

	Women		Men	
Ages (years)	1979	2019	1979	2019
USA				
Before 65	26%	20%	40%	31%
65 to 84	50%	41%	49%	46%
85+	24%	39%	11%	23%
England and Wales				
Before 65	17%	13%	29%	19%
65 to 84	59%	39%	61%	49%
85+	24%	48%	10%	32%

Sources: US: National Center for Health Statistics; UK (England and Wales): Office for National Statistics

the elderly in the United States and the UK who live into their late eighties or beyond.

Life expectancy is no more than today's best estimate of the average of a wide range of plausible lifespans. Average life expectancy will be a useful guide for an insurance company that can spread its exposure across many individuals. Self-insurance of longevity risk is not efficient for individuals, no matter how deep their pockets. Self-insurance of mortality risk will naturally push individuals towards excessive saving and a lower standard of living, and towards the diminished estates or penury for the minority who live to great old age.

Table 3.2 gives some broad measures, based on US and UK data, for how long retirements starting at age 65 may now be expected to last. It suggests that half of American women will live at least 22 years beyond their 65th birthday, and that one in ten American

TABLE 3.2 **How long might my retirement last?**
In years, assuming retirement from age 65 for both men and women in around 2021

UK data	Average	1 in 4 chance	1 in 10 chance
Men	20	27	31
Women	22	29	33
US data	**Average**	**1 in 4 chance**	**1 in 10 chance**
Men	19	26	31
Women	22	29	33
Couple (both 65)	27	31	35

Sources: US: Data derived from US Social Security Administration longevity visualiser tool; average data for couple show expected 50th percentile. UK (England and Wales): Office for National Statistics, life expectancy calculator. Calculations underlying US and UK data may not be directly comparable.

women will live at least 33 years beyond their 65th birthday (that is, to age 98), with comparable figures in the UK.

There are numerous websites that fine-tune the national data to take account of self-reported personal characteristics such as current age, lifestyle, health, gender and ethnicity. However, from a financial planning perspective, the key message is the great uncertainty of the length of retirement. The data suggest that more than half of American men aged 65 will die before reaching age 85, but there is also a 10% chance that a joint pension intended to provide for a couple, both aged 65, will be needed to pay out a regular income for 35 years – in other words, until age 100.

A significant minority of pensioners will therefore need to stretch their pension savings over more than 30 years. For the wealthy this may not be a problem. But for most pensioners, it is a tall order for life savings accumulated over working careers of 45 years, if that long.

Reducing risk in old age: a role for life annuities?

It is normally misguided to self-insure big risks. Extreme weather conditions generate news stories of the financial misfortune of individuals who either choose not to or cannot obtain insurance for their homes. It is almost never sensible for an individual deliberately to save on paying a modest annual premium (if it is) and forgo the assurance of being made good in the event of an unlikely but catastrophic financial loss.

One aspect of the retirement challenge is the choice between drawing an income from your investments, the value of which will fluctuate with financial markets, and alternatively paying insurance companies a lump sum in exchange for a life annuity, which provides a regular income for the remainder of your life. Table 3.2 gives an indication of the uncertainty surrounding the length of an individual's or a couple's retirement. The risk of financial ruin (as a result of outlasting one's savings) by self-insuring this uncertainty can be large. The financial management of a 75-year-old who continues (as most do) to rely on drawing down regular instalments from their pension savings has been compared to a volatile strategy of investing 100% of their retirement savings in the stock market.[2]

The financial burden of unusually long retirements makes this a natural marketplace for insurance companies. They routinely insure this risk by selling life annuities that guarantee an income for life. Typically, this will be a fixed, regular amount or increase at a pre-set rate to offset gradual erosion by inflation (and it can be linked formally to inflation).

Many will pass up this opportunity because they are pessimistic about their own life chances and because they think it unfair that the insurer profits if the pensioner dies early. In short, they often expect that a life annuity would be a waste of money. However, enhanced annuities for those with poor life chances may be available and there is evidence that education about the nature of insurance contracts may improve their take-up.

Rejecting the option to buy an annuity, with at least part of pension savings, risks burdening many pensioners' loved ones if they do reach great old age. The wealthy may reject the option of purchasing a life annuity because they have plenty of money and in the next breath they might say that they intend to leave the residue of their estate to their loved ones or to good causes. In effect, they are asking their estate to underwrite their own mortality risk.

Actuaries and financial economists are particularly attracted by insurance policies which take this longevity risk away from the individual.[3] Self-insurance ties up personal resources in excessive precautionary saving and reduces potential spending (and the standard of living) in retirement. The ideal policy for many economists and actuaries is a deferred inflation-linked annuity, which protects the individual against the twin financial risks of a very lengthy retirement and cumulative inflation.

To some extent, this is already widely available. Mitigation of longevity and inflation risk can be provided by taking advantage of options to defer, and so increase from a later start date, entitlements to regular, inflation-linked payments of social security in the United States and state old-age pensions in the UK. For many, this will provide the best way to reduce uncertainty of their standard of living in old age or of the estates that they can bequeath.

In the United States, insurance companies offer deferred annuities that start making payouts at a specified date in the future, and these can be available with various options, including joint life policies for couples and fixed annual rate of increase to allow for expected inflation. (These annuities do not normally include formal inflation linking.) An academic report published in 2020 called deferred income annuities "a low-cost way to hedge the risk of outliving one's assets".

The report said that those on the cusp of retirement, with typical life expectancy, would optimally commit at age 65 about 8–15% of their pension pot to a deferred income annuity that begins paying out at age 85. Although the research took account of inflation, investors would need to consider how inflation risk impacted the appeal of the deferred annuity compared with other investment allocations.

For many investors, loss aversion will make them particularly reluctant to make a substantial investment which would carry the risk of a total loss if they die, as half would be expected to do, before age 85. Many investors would conclude the deferred annuity feels much too expensive.

Saving in old age

One counter-intuitive finding of research into the finances of the elderly is that they continue to save out of their income. This has been found by different studies from various countries and applies to all age groups and all income levels. Although this pattern of saving by the elderly is consistent with risk aversion increasing with age, academics disagree about whether attitudes to risk do materially change with age.

For many, saving in old age will include precautionary saving, or self-insurance, to meet the potential burden of end-of-life care expenses. The elderly are presumably not concerned with being able to meet the average health and care costs of old age, which they are unlikely to know much about. They are more likely to be concerned, having heard the anecdotes of friends and family, with the risk of incurring much larger costs of end-of-life care.

A 2017 report based on 18 years of detailed data on nursing-home use in the United States and associated out-of-pocket expenses for families, weighted to represent the US population over the age of 50, found that one in 20 elderly Americans spends more than four years in a nursing home.[4] But this is not the typical experience. Half of elderly Americans spend a total of ten days or less during their lifetimes in a nursing home (for example, in rehabilitative care following a stay in hospital). Many of the elderly avoid the cost of long-term care, but for a minority long-term care represents a major financial burden.

In the UK the 2011 Dilnot Commission on funding social care found a similar pattern, with large costs inflicted on a significant minority. In the UK in 2011, about 10% of older people faced care costs of over £100,000 and they faced around a 1 in 20 chance of costs of £150,000 or more. However, about a quarter faced no extra costs. Dilnot concluded: "People do not know what their lifetime costs will be, so they all face the possibility of very high lifetime costs. A risk-averse person would want to plan for the worst case."

How much income can I draw?

Over an average working life, which often spans four or more decades, income uncertainty from year to year is a given. Earnings and careers progress or suffer greater or lesser setbacks so there is no certainty from one year to the next.

In pension terms, certainty was offered by old-style final-salary company (or government sector) pensions, where employers assumed responsibility for paying former employees' contractual pensions for the remainder of their lives. However, income certainty comes at a heavy price. Pensioners who pay an insurer a large lump sum in exchange for receiving a regular annuity for the rest of their lives, sometimes approaching the length of time they were at work, pay dearly for this assurance.

Easy-to-find online annuity calculators give ready estimates of the income that could be generated from an investment fund. These amounts increase with interest rates. In June 2022, for example, these indicated that a 65-year-old in the United States might get from an insurance company an annual fixed income of around $58,000 in exchange for a one-off payment of US $1,000,000; whereas in the UK in exchange for £1,000,000 an insurance company might provide a pension of just over £70,000. This difference reflects variations in interest rates as well as differences in life expectancy and other factors.

These incomes will erode over time with inflation, which remains a major risk for many cautious pensioners. Monetary policy in developed countries commonly targets price stability, which the US Federal Reserve defines as an average of 2% per year. If an American couple live for 35 years after first drawing a level life pension, the value of that pension would have halved if the Fed meets its price stability objective (see Table 3.3). If it fails, and at the time of publication, the Fed together with all other leading central banks were presiding over inflation substantially in excess of their formal targets (of around 2%), the pension would be worth very much less.

TABLE 3.3 **The corrosive impact of modest inflation on fixed pensions**
US$, £ or €

$/£/€50,000 is worth after:		10 years	20 years	30 years	35 years
	1%	45,264	40,977	37,096	35,296
Average annual inflation:	2%	41,017	33,649	27,604	25,001
	3%	37,205	27,684	20,599	17,769
	4%	33,778	22,819	15,416	12,671

Source: Authors' calculations

The potential annual payments from a fixed annuity and separately from an inflation-linked life annuity, though rarely selected, provide valuable benchmarks against which to assess the normally less secure income projected in a financial plan prepared by an adviser. In practice, financial advisers commonly back-test model **asset allocations** from stocks and bonds to show an approximate safe withdrawal rate, which could, with hindsight, have provided a sustainable level of income, growing through time to match inflation.

An early example of this was an article from 1994 by William Bengen, a former US financial planner, whose research led to what became known as the 4% rule.[5] Based on available US historical market returns, Bengen calculated that a pensioner aged 65 should be able to withdraw an amount equivalent to 4% of their pension savings (assumed to be invested equally in stocks and government bonds), and that this amount in dollars could then be indexed to inflation and drawn down each year over a retirement of 30 years.

This model has been tested and reappraised extensively since then (not least by Bengen himself), making use of a longer data set and greater availability of international data. However, academics have noted that Bengen was proposing to finance a constant, non-volatile spending plan using a risky, volatile investment strategy.

Bengen had used the longest run of data on US market returns then available to him, from 1926 to 1992, a total of 66 years. Despite being able to construct a reasonable number of overlapping 30-year periods (his principal chosen length of retirement), he only had two distinct 30-year periods, which is not a big dataset. The 4% inflation-linked drawdown rule has played a powerful role in anchoring expectations for pension income ever since.

It is unavoidable that pensioners will be attracted to the shortcut of a simple rule to benchmark an affordable pension. In drawing lessons from history, investors need to ask whether the historical record may be a misleading guide to the future.

By the early 2020s, for example, low interest rates had lifted returns generated from stocks, bonds and almost all other assets. A reasonable expectation is that prospective returns have been reduced and that the past performance of balanced holdings of equities and especially bonds are a particularly poor guide to future returns (see Chapter 4). Personal pensions cannot appeal to historical market experience to suggest that, going forward, risk-taking is less than it is.

The attention of advisers and investors is often focused on managing the mismatch between drawing a stable pension and the volatility of the investments that often fund the pension. The dangers include the damaging impact on living standards of selling investments when investment values are lower than was assumed in a financial plan. Equally, there can be gains when investments are sold at higher prices than was assumed.

Planners often call this "sequence risk" and emphasise the importance of regular reassessment of the financial plan and, if necessary, the pension payment, as time passes. Advisers commonly recommend building a buffer of liquidity to ensure that a few years' projected drawdowns can be met from investment income and cash holdings. This can help manage sequence risk, as it reduces the initial need to sell assets at depressed prices in bad times.

To a financial economist, this looks like a naïve policy of relying on a short-term bounce in markets to restore the solvency of a financial plan that was agreed in better times. The undoubted advantage of a buffer of cash to meet near-term needs, whatever happens in markets, is that it facilitates hand-holding by advisers and allows for time to reflect and consider different options. It also improves the likelihood that a temporary spike of illiquidity, which raises trading costs, will correct itself. Of course, depressed market valuations might also recover in time to help a plan.

A fundamental problem with both the 4% rule and the economist's inflation-linked life annuity is that a stable real income during retirement often will not meet the financial needs or preferences of retirees.

As we've seen, a need to consider provision for possible long-term care costs is a reality for pensioners. Likewise, retirees tend to spend more in the early years of retirement than in later years. Research published in 2022 by the French business school EDHEC, in conjunction with Bank of America, models a formulation for the risk of long-term care needs with a "glide path" or plan for selling investments and adjusting investment allocations which responds, within limits, to changes in market conditions.[6] It suggests, in effect, that the pension drawn each year should adjust as new relevant information is revealed. They report that this leads to better results than a fixed drawdown rule for almost all levels of risk-taking by the pensioner. It does this by limiting drawdowns in bad financial times, which may reflect poor market conditions or unexpected increases in longevity.

Investors need to decide how far to move away from the expensive and illiquid insurance route; a decision to buy a simple life annuity cannot be reversed. They can retain a greater degree of control and flexibility over their wealth when they choose to hold a range of investments to support their pension plan. It gives them options to respond to changing needs.

However, having more opportunities comes with the risk of an unanticipated depletion of resources and even the possibility of money running out. We discuss how to structure managed investments when seeking a secure retirement income in the following chapters. No one needs to allocate all their financial savings to a life annuity, but retirees ought to consider how they can help manage longevity and investment market risk.[7]

What drives performance?

If you see easy money to be made in the stock market or anywhere else, you have not looked hard enough

In times of acute crisis, government bonds are still the investor's best friend. But over time, they are always vulnerable to inflation

Remember Robinhood, the user-friendly online trading platform? During the pandemic, the ease of accessing online trading with Robinhood and its competitors enabled the phenomenon of the crowd-promoted **meme stock**.

The standard-bearing early meme stock was the equity of GameStop Corp, the world's largest video game retailer. This was widely purchased by great numbers of loyal individual or retail investors in early 2021 but the business was regarded by many traditional analysts as a laggard in transitioning to digital downloads from disc games and to an online rather than a bricks and mortar presence. The stock itself had been "shorted" by a number of traditional hedge funds. In other words, these hedge funds borrowed and then sold stock they did not own, expecting to be able to buy it back at a later lower price.

The battalions of retail investors in GameStop overpowered the short-selling professionals, who, being victims of a classic squeeze, needed to buy the stock rapidly and in volume to limit their losses. Meanwhile, in the dog-eat-dog world of money management, trend-following hedge funds were seen to follow the retail investors in ramping up the price of GameStop. This worsened the plight of the valuation-conscious, short-selling hedge funds, which incurred substantial losses.

The buying frenzy led the GameStop share price to surge 17-fold in January 2021. The company then took advantage of the newfound popularity of its equity to strengthen its financial position by raising $1.5 billion in new funding. An army of social-media-savvy traders was seen to have upended the best-laid plans of short-selling hedge funds. Not quite taking from the rich and giving to the poor, but near enough.

Meme stocks and lottery stocks are interesting for two very different reasons. Lottery stocks are volatile equities that are thought to offer the opportunity of outsized gains. Typically, lottery stocks represent companies that are exploiting disruptive new technologies; they are quite likely to fail, but they may encounter spectacular success.

As with any lottery, success is clear with hindsight, but sober reflection suggests that investors should expect disappointment even while they hope for a runaway success. The evidence that exists, whether for full time day traders or opportunistic stock selectors, is that retail investors who trade individual stocks typically underperform a buy-and-hold approach to the broad equity market.[1]

It is no surprise that so few make a career from day trading: underperformance soon becomes unsupportable. Investors might think that their carefully selected concentrated stock portfolio ought to have at least an even chance of performing as well as the broader market, whether they are as skilled as they think or not. It turns out that this widely held view is wrong.

The performance of the stock market itself is dragged up and skewed by the exceptional cumulative performance of a small number of stocks. These are probably the type of stocks which entice the individual investors to become active investors.

A 2018 article found that most US equities underperform US **Treasury bills**, while the positively skewed performance of the small minority of superior performers compounds over time to provide the outperformance (known as the equity **risk premium**) for the overall stock market.[2]

It concluded that "while the overall US stock market has handily outperformed Treasury bills in the long run, most individual common stocks have not". This is the undoing of many active investors. The dice are loaded against them, even before allowing for fees or the mundane necessity of earning a living.

The tortoise of a broad market exposure (which is exciting enough for many investors) is a surer way to manage wealth than to try to pre-empt the latest new thing by buying before its stock price appreciates. Sometimes investors need to be agile when investing, but most of the time it is better to ride with the broad market.

So far this century, investors have been buffeted by three major equity market setbacks, starting with the unwinding in 2000–2 of the "irrational exuberance" of the end-of-20th-century telecom, media and technology boom. The next major setback, which was much more widespread, was the global financial crisis of 2007–9. The third was the sharp initial response to the covid-19 pandemic in early 2020, and a fourth was in progress as this book went to press in 2022.

Through these crises, government bonds became increasingly expensive and for years – until 2022 – have offered yields that struggle to cover advisers' fees, let alone to provide a decent income for investors. These developments reset the climate for managing savings and wealth towards expecting less favourable stock market returns and for modest returns to be earned from creditworthy government bonds. Above all, these developments raised the cost of providing a secure regular income.

Traditionally, domestic **Treasury bonds** and bills have been considered free from credit risk and to be safe harbours for investors. This is reinforced when governments can print their own money, which they can do if they have their own currency. This has been a cornerstone of much modern portfolio theory and practice. It was shaken by government debt crises that followed the credit crunch of 2007–9, especially within the euro zone, where individual countries have voluntarily given up their own ability to control their national currencies opting instead for the wider monetary discipline of the euro zone. The previous inflation risk of Greece, Italy and other euro zone countries was replaced with a new emphasis on their credit risk.

The disappearance of reliable recurring interest income from government bonds due to low interest rates posed severe challenges for cautious investors. An unwelcome degree of risk-taking and uncertainty about the standard of living became unavoidable as the security of income from government bonds became too expensive for many. In this environment, many financial advisers looked for alternative investments to anchor investment strategies because Treasury bonds first offered so little income and then inflicted capital losses on investors when yields increased. But despite the allure of the stock market, government bonds remain an important ingredient of most properly diversified investment portfolios.

Safe harbours that provide different kinds of shelter

If investors take no risk, they should not expect to receive a premium return. But one investor's **safe harbour** may be a risky investment for another.

For a short-term investor, domestic Treasury bills represent the minimum-risk investment that protects capital values in the short-term, and they provide a guaranteed but typically modest short-term return. In an environment of low and stable inflation, domestic Treasury bonds give security for the lifetime of the bond. Treasury bills that mature every three or six months are risky for this purpose, as they are immediately vulnerable to cyclical variations in interest rates as prospects for the economy fluctuate. A Treasury bond, if held to maturity, avoids this risk and guarantees a return over the life of the bond (except that, as we'll see below, the interest income from the bond may have to be reinvested at lower yields).

The major risk for Treasury bonds is that inflation increases. Some economists argue that the periods of high and variable inflation in the 20th century (in particular, the 25 years before 1990) were an anomaly and that the era of central bank independence since then may have more in common with the earlier gold standard era in terms of stability of inflation expectations.[3] Whether this can be relied upon in the decades ahead is discussed in Chapter 7.

An investor who wants a secure income that is also protected against inflation can use inflation-linked bonds (also known as Treasury inflation-protected securities or TIPS, linkers or real bonds). An individual inflation-linked bond should provide a match for a known set of future payments linked to inflation. A linker would provide the low-risk (but expensive) means to insure against adverse inflation and adverse real interest-rate surprises if it is held to maturity.

Before maturity, inflation-linked bonds do not provide a reliable hedge against inflation surprises and may temporarily fall in value if an increase in inflation is accompanied by a rise in **real interest rates**. Andrew Ang, formerly Ann F. Kaplan Professor of Business at Columbia Business School, summarises their role by saying that "real bonds are lousy inflation hedges" and he finds that the short-term relationship (correlation) between the performance of inflation-linked bonds and inflation is close to zero.

This is partly because the real yields on inflation-linked bonds are themselves volatile. In addition, the illiquidity of inflation-linked markets further undermines their attraction. Despite this, when investors hold the inflation-linked bonds to maturity, they will provide the inflation-linked yield that was promised when they were purchased.

Which government bonds will perform best?

The **yield curve** describes how the rate of interest paid by the government on Treasury bills (that is, cash) compares with the rate paid by the government on its longer-term Treasury bonds. Table 4.1 explains the difference between the two.

TABLE 4.1 **Treasury bills and Treasury bonds**

Treasury bill	Government debt with less than one year's original maturity (typically between one and six months). Treasury bills are regarded as an investment in risk-free cash
Treasury bond	Government debt with more than one year's original maturity. In designing broad investment strategies, it is conventional to treat a government bond with a remaining maturity of less than 12 months as if it were a Treasury bill. In the United States, Treasury debts with between one and ten years' original maturity are called "notes". In this book, the expression "Treasury bond" refers to any Treasury security of more than one year's maturity

This relationship is important for how the financial markets assess different risks, including inflation and the likelihood of a recession. An insurance company does not need to be paid a premium yield by the taxpayer to be persuaded to hold Treasury bonds, nor does the pensioner need a premium return to hold inflation-linked government bonds. This means that it is unclear how much premium return, if any, should be expected from government bonds, whether indexed or not, over cash.

The normal shape of the yield curve has been an area of extensive, and often inconclusive, macroeconomic research. The pattern over the past century or more is clear on two things. First, historically, there has normally been an upward-sloping yield curve: Treasury bonds have offered higher yields and returns than Treasury bills or cash. Also, long-dated Treasury bonds have typically offered a higher yield than shorter-dated Treasury bonds (this is known as the "term premium").

For example, in its 2022 report, Credit Suisse reports that in virtually all countries with available data going back to 1900, longer-dated government bonds have provided a higher return than Treasury bills.[4] This premium return averaged 1.3% for the United States and 0.9% for the UK.

The extent of this premium varies over time, and at least in recent decades, the pattern has been similar in the major markets. The term premium is often explained as the additional reward that short-term investors need to be offered to tempt them to buy longer-dated bonds because such bonds are subject to price volatility. However, the relationship is more complicated.

First, longer-dated bonds are not riskier for all investors; they can be low risk for any long-term investor who confidently expects inflation to stay low. Also, investors may wish to hold government bonds because they are typically the best and most liquid diversifier of equity market risk during market crises.

There is also a bigger picture. The emergence of the great inflation of the second half of the 20th century, and its subsequent mastering by central banks and governments, makes it hazardous to conclude that long-dated government bonds should be expected to offer a higher yield than cash (but see Chapter 7).

The exposure of bond yields to macroeconomic risk factors has been suggested as an alternative explanation for the likely relationship between long-term and short-term interest rates on government debt. Inflation and inflation risk (that is, uncertainty about future inflation rates) are prime determinants of long-term bond yields. When there is more confidence in central banks and governments in controlling inflation, uncertainty will be lower. As a result, deposit rates and government bond yields will be similar; in other words, the yield curve will probably be flatter.

Superimposed on this is the impact of central bank efforts to manage the impact of the business cycle, typically by lowering short rates at the start of a recession and raising them as the economy approaches full capacity. Since the global financial crisis after 2007, the picture has become yet more muddied. The enormous central bank purchases of government debt, and also corporate bonds, which became known as quantitative easing, have at times been an overwhelming influence as central banks strove to provide markets with additional liquidity.

Inflation-linked government bonds offer lower yields than conventional government bonds. The difference between the two is commonly described as the **break-even rate of inflation**. This is the future inflation rate at which indexation on the inflation linked bond offsets the higher yield from the **conventional bond**. The break-even rate of inflation is often used as the market's expectation for future inflation.

In practice, various issues obscure the picture. This includes the extent of uncertainty about that future rate of inflation. Offsetting this, inflation-linked bond yields may contain a premium to compensate for their comparative illiquidity. This premium is likely to vary over time. An important detail is that regulations for tax-exempt pension funds and insurance companies can also cause concentrations of demand for particular segments of the conventional and inflation-linked markets. These can lead to valuation anomalies which require particularly long-time horizons to exploit. Biases in the measure of inflation used for index linked bonds has been a particularly pronounced issue in the UK.[5]

These factors hinder simple interpretation of the break-even rate as an inflation forecast. Nevertheless, the break-even rate is a readily available, crude rule of thumb for a market forecast of inflation. If a long-term investor has strong views that differ from the apparent market rate of inflation, these views can influence whether the investor decides to include inflation-linked bonds or conventional bonds in implementing strategy. Investors whose safe-harbour investment is an inflation-linked government bond should have a strategic position in conventional government bonds if they expect conventional bonds to provide an adequate reward for expected inflation, including a margin for uncertainty.

In conclusion, the terms on which creditworthy governments borrow still provide the cornerstone foundation for modelling investment strategies. This can be summarised as follows:

■ Inflation-linked government bonds can provide a benchmark for long-term investors, whose financial objectives vary over time with inflation.

■ Treasury bills provide a benchmark for short-term investors, whose objectives are more immediate and measured in today's prices.

■ It is reasonable to assume that inflation-linked bonds will provide a modest illiquidity premium return over Treasury bills in the medium term.

■ The most cautious long-term investors may have an anchor holding of inflation-linked bonds. More commonly, and especially at times of lesser inflation uncertainty, high-quality conventional bonds replace inflation-linked bonds as the core holdings of long-term investors. This reflects both their greater liquidity, a possible **inflation risk premium** and the convenience of their greater regular income distribution.

The equity risk premium

The Triumph of the Optimists is the title that Dimson, Marsh and Staunton gave their path-breaking review of returns from stocks, bonds and cash in 17 countries since 1900. Their message was that equity investors had done better than they could reasonably have hoped since the start of the 20th century, and they should expect the 21st century to be less generous for long-term equity investors.

The original research has since been extended to 21 countries with continuous stock market histories (and 14 countries with shorter track records) and updated annually, most recently in the 2022 *Credit Suisse Global Investment Returns Yearbook*. Over more recent decades, government bond returns have, until 2022, seemed to be unsustainably strong and stock market (and other asset) returns were pulled along in the slipstream of increasingly more expensive bond markets. This resulted in a prolonged period of outperformance of stock markets by longer-dated government bonds. This was despite equity markets being lifted by the wave of stock market champions who led internet-based innovation.

Overall, in the first two decades of this century, equities continued to perform well relative to cash, despite the three major setbacks described earlier. Any one of these major stock market crises could easily have wrong-footed an underdiversified investor who took as normal the good times that persisted in the years leading up to each of these major market declines.

So, what performance should equity investors expect and how does it relate to the likely performance from bonds and cash? This is an area of great controversy and therefore uncertainty. It's an uncertainty that needs to be reflected in the design of any investment strategy.

The starting point is history, for which thanks to the work of Dimson, Marsh and Staunton, now extends to cover effectively all national stock markets. The longest data series show conclusively that, over long periods of years, outperformance by equities, especially of cash, has been the norm and risk-taking has eventually been rewarded.

The history of financial markets shows that this pattern of equity outperformance has sometimes taken a long time to assert itself. There have been long periods when equities have not outperformed cash and, especially, bonds. This applies not only to individual small markets, which are not well diversified, but also to the United States and the rest of the world.

So much for the past: what matters for setting an investment strategy is what we expect for the future. The majority view remains that financial market history of the 20th century was kinder to equity investors than they could reasonably have expected. The years ahead, on average, are likely to be less generous in absolute terms, though most analysts would expect equities to outperform bonds over the decades to come. Translating this into expectations for the future is impeded by disagreements about the normal or equilibrium level of the market, for example in relation to company earnings or interest rates.

This discussion typically focuses on expectations for market returns and economic risk factors. The stock market is built up from individual companies and industries, and times of rapid technological change are typically heralded by an appreciation in the share prices of the firms the market thinks are best placed to exploit the new technologies. In the early 20th century, examples included Ford Motor Company with the mass production of cars, and Radio Corporation of America (RCA) with early radio. In the late 1960s, the "nifty-fifty" growth stocks included Coca-Cola, Eastman Kodak, McDonalds and Philip Morris. The late 1990s had the dotcom bubble.

More recently, the wave of web-based industrial transformation has driven the United States and, to a lesser extent, other stock markets. This has featured some of the same firms as the dotcom era, but most are now household names including Microsoft and Tesla, as well as the FAANG stocks of Facebook (whose listed parent is Meta Platforms Inc), Amazon, Apple, Netflix and Google (whose listed parent is Alphabet) and Taiwan Semiconductor Manufacturing Company (TSMC). Hindsight makes it easy to identify corporate winners, but the message for private investors is that it is best not to take a bet on which individual stocks will be tomorrow's stock market darlings, but instead to go with the flow of a diversified strategy.

There is agreement that the equity risk premium is likely to change, for example if the economy experiences widespread technological change, or even if the amount of wealth available to be invested changes. But there is no consensus to tell us how it might change when economic conditions change.

One version of this is that stock market prices fluctuate randomly or, in the jargon, follow a random walk so that high returns could be followed by high or low returns without any predictability. An alternative view is that we might look for valuations of the stock market to be pulled back towards the average from the past (see Chapter 5). If this is true, then if investment returns have been above average, they are likely subsequently to come down, and if they have been below average, they are likely to increase. This process of overreaction, where good market performance is expected to be followed by poorer performance, is called **mean reversion**.

Others suggest that we should expect the stock market to be priced higher in the 21st century than on average in the past. This is because investors can now easily invest at less risk and by paying lower fees because of the wider use of well-diversified investment funds, and especially of low-fee index funds and well-diversified exchange traded funds (**ETF**s). As investors can access the market less expensively, this makes it more attractive to invest.

Prior to 2022 there was broad consensus that bond returns had in recent decades been unsustainable. In essence, as yields were driven to historically low levels, it became implausible that yields would fall as far as in the past, and so bond performance would be disappointing in future (see Chapter 5). This might be because bond yields recover and so prices fall (as in 2022), or because yields will in future vary with the business cycle but be anchored around a lower normal level than prior to 2008. This remains a source of major uncertainty.

At the start of the 21st century, finance experts differed on prospects for the premium return that should be expected from equity investing. These differences show no sign of abating. There is increasing agreement (but not consensus) that medium-term prospects need to take some account of whether the market is cheap or expensive at the outset. A variation on this is that, as market risk fluctuates, investors should want and expect a higher risk premium when the market is more volatile. This may coincide with times that the market is less expensive, but it might not.

This sounds like common sense, but there is also agreement that it is difficult to exploit valuation indicators to earn higher returns. There would be quite wide support for the idea that it is fruitless to adjust expectations for the equity risk premium used in long-term planning except when the stock market appears to be either unusually expensive or unusually cheap.

Researchers who believe that the stock market is expensive give lower estimates of future returns. There is increasing agreement that, at some times, the risk premium may be higher than at other times. In 2011, Rob Arnott, chairman of Research Affiliates, an investment manager, wrote that:

> this brief history lesson illuminates that the much-vaunted 4–5% risk premium for stocks is unreliable and a dangerous assumption on which to make our future plans. In our view, a more normal economic environment would suggest 2–3%, which is the historic risk premium absent the rise in valuation multiples in the past 30 years.

In their 2022 report, Dimson, Marsh and Staunton, took a different approach and suggested that investors should factor into their long-term thinking and modelling an annualised equity premium relative to cash of about 3.5% for world equities.

This is a consistent view they have held throughout this millennium. In 2021, they added (while leaving the expected premium returns unchanged) that a balanced portfolio of 70% equity/30% bond offered a return of about 2% ahead of inflation. Although they expect the equity return to be markedly ahead of inflation, this level of returns for a balanced fund is nevertheless "about a third of the real return enjoyed by the previous three generations. Many savers, investors, pension plans and institutions are challenged by the low-return world." Meanwhile, the greatly reduced costs of trading may lead to more speculation and so more volatility.

Debate about future average equity market performance has little effect on the likelihood of next year's equity market performance being disappointing. It does have a large impact on the prospects for wealth accumulation from equities over extended periods. In this tougher environment, the one thing any investor can do to raise their expected returns is to be vigilant about the fees that they pay. This always has a large impact on wealth accumulation over extended periods of time.

Equity risk: don't bank on time diversifying risk

The size of the equity risk premium would be of less concern if it was true that equities are less risky for long-term investors than for short-term investors. This is a separate area of debate with strong differences of opinion – and therefore much confusion – among investors.

The longer the time horizon, the more likely it is that stock market indices will outperform bonds or cash, simply because, on average, stocks are expected to perform better. Furthermore, the longer the period, the more likely it is that this cumulative outperformance will translate into an increasingly large proportion of the initial investment. Long-term investors in equities should expect to do better on average than investors in bonds or cash. The longer the time period, the better in monetary terms they should expect, on average, to do. So long as equity investors are offered a positive risk premium, which more than outweighs the extra investment management fees they pay, this should be uncontroversial.

The real issue is the risk of disappointing results over longer periods of time; how this can compound into an increasingly large shortfall; and how strongly investors should want to avoid the pain (if any) caused by such shortfalls. This has always been a central focus of finance, and it has been brought into even sharper focus through the understanding of loss aversion in behavioural finance (see Chapter 2).

As already discussed, for periods of a decade or more, the risk of equities underperforming long-term bonds and cash is not negligible. This risk persists even though equities are, on average, expected to outperform bonds and cash by a wide cumulative margin.

Nevertheless, in recent years, there has been growing agreement that the standard statistical assumptions which frequently underly wealth-planning exercises understate short-term risk (crashes happen more often than the models assume) and may overstate long-term equity risk. This is because a body of academic research supports the widely held view that, to some extent, markets do overreact and mean-revert. As a result, equity markets vary less over time than traditional models would suggest.

If this is true, stock market volatility measured over, say, decades or 20-year periods would be less than would be expected if we were simply to extrapolate short-term volatility. However, the degree to which this is the case is controversial, particularly among academic researchers.

The simple, easy-to-use models that underpin many savings planning exercises have been widely criticised. But these approaches continue to be used, partly because there is no agreement on how to replace them. However, the weakness of these models needs to be considered when planning an investment strategy.

An expectation that a risk-based strategy is likely, but not certain, to achieve an objective is often reassuring enough. If investors want more certainty (see Chapter 2), the underlying investment strategy needs to be based, in so far as it is possible, by buying a fixed or inflation-linked annuity from an insurance company or trying to match (or hedge) their expected expenditure using tailored inflation-linked or conventional government bonds. Often the truth is that the price of such insurance is too high, and many investors have little choice but to live with a significant degree of uncertainty.

At present, the best guide to the risk of equities underperforming cash or bonds is given by examining the historical data. As discussed, the prevailing view of finance academics is that the 21st century is likely to be less favourable to equity markets than the 20th century was. So, a reasonable assumption would be that the incidence of disappointing equity markets will be higher in the 21st century than it was in the 20th.

The first two decades were certainly consistent with this. As recent experience shows, the risk of equity strategies underperforming safe-harbour investment strategies over long periods needs to be taken seriously. These are not remote events to be dismissed as exceptional bad luck: these things happen.

Finally, as already mentioned, the notion that the equity risk premium is a constant – whether it is 3% or 6% – is open to question. The presence of mean reversion in the equity market would suggest that expected market returns can vary. This insight, though, is much more easily agreed than exploited.

Manager performance

Star managers don't walk on water

Campbell Harvey, the J. Paul Sticht Professor of Finance at Duke University, urged investors in a 2021 article to "Be skeptical of asset management research". In it, Harvey highlighted the incentives facing investment researchers to come up with good results. Disappointing or inconclusive results do not help promote careers nor do they sell investment products. This leads to bias in reported results since the formulations that produced fewer promising results are generally kept out of sight.

The characteristic human weaknesses of wishful thinking and confirmation bias can affect any of us, and evidence of this bias affecting results need not be due to dishonourable practice, though it may reflect poor practice. Harvey reported that he found articles in leading finance journals that give evidence of 400 strategies that are supposed to beat the market. These published research findings are then used as the basis for new investment strategies that are sold to investors. Often, they disappoint.

Have I got a winning strategy for you? Probably not.

The choice of manager often seems critical to both individual and institutional investors. One of the most difficult tasks for an investor is to distinguish luck or **noise** from skill when presented with a track record which shows historic outperformance.

Noise is introduced to investment performance by unskillful managers of investors' portfolios. It is often (erroneously) described as "alpha" when it is positive, although sceptics have described alpha as "the average error term". There are always likely to be more unskilled noise managers with marketable track records than skilled managers who, in addition to being skilled, have a marketable record at any point in time. Noise will normally bring some extra volatility; it will also incur fees and distract investors, thus wasting valuable time and, probably, money.

From time to time there have been much-lauded star money managers whose performance and reputation disappoints either slowly over time or surprisingly quickly. These incidents seem likely to encourage mistrust of experts and greater reliance on self-managed investment accounts. In turn, the popularity of self-investment probably has much to do with the preferences of those who (to the puzzlement of others) find it fun to trade for themselves. Why trust a money manager when you can do it yourself for less, and have fun and an online social life as well?

There are, however, circumstances where the difference from the market performance is likely to be small. In this case, buying a market-matching exchange traded fund or index fund, which typically has low costs, may be an easier decision to justify than a combination of managers, who when added together closely match the market index. This applies when the market is efficient and there are few opportunities for **active management**. It also seems to apply more often than active managers would admit.

Many experts, whose independence means that they have no "skin in the game", have over the decades concluded that to seek a manager who will outperform in the future is like trying to find a needle in a haystack. In the words of the Nobel laureate in economics, the late Paul A. Samuelson, "Perhaps there really are managers who can outperform the market consistently – logic would suggest that they exist. But they are remarkably well hidden."

Investors are often happy to get higher returns, however they are gained. However, financially literate investors should get an indication of how much risk the fund has taken with their money – for example, calculating the excess return or risk premium of the fund divided by the risk of the fund (often measured as a **standard deviation**).

Such a ratio, which has many names and forms including the **Sharpe ratio**, the information ratio, and the Sortino ratio, can be a sensible way to consider risk-adjusted performance (subject to the important proviso that the underlying investments are liquid; see Chapter 7). These ratios have the added benefit that they need only know the return histories of the fund and the benchmark to calculate quantities. It is then incumbent on investors or their advisers to judge whether the return history fully reflects the risk characteristics that are embedded within the fund.

We know of no strategy that has shown such superficially attractive risk-adjusted returns as the fraudulent track record of the Madoff fraud. Correspondingly, perfectly honourable strategies may include elements of optionality for which investors should expect, most of the time, to receive a steady stream of extra performance which is offset by occasional sharp losses of value.

It is easy to group together some types of hedge funds which have this characteristic. Chapter 9 also discusses ways in which credit portfolios also can be expected to perform surprisingly poorly in bad times. For such funds, the use of historic return patterns to anticipate future return profiles is not appropriate, unless the fund's history includes such bad times. When a new fund is brought to market, this is unlikely, or at least needs checking. Sometimes we know why the past may be a particularly poor guide to the future.

The ability of an investment manager to perform and manage risks relative to a benchmark is one aspect of managing wealth.

For many investors other aspects of wealth management are increasingly important. This includes ensuring that the investments are aligned with their owners' ethical, social and governance views, which is discussed further in Chapter 8. There are further issues in the context of the broader role of financial planning advice (Chapter 2) and of providing pension income (Chapter 3).

Managing wealth is about much more than beating an index. It's concerning that accountability for performance outcomes quickly becomes muddled as investors seek to accommodate a wider range objectives and preferences. How investors should combine the different sources of investment return in ways that try to balance their hopes for good performance with their tolerance for disappointment is discussed in the following chapters.

Inflation, interest rates, booms and busts: is anything safe?

*When investing for the long term, it is
better to be a tortoise than a hare*

*We don't believe anyone knows where interest rates and
inflation will be in 15 years' time, and this matters*

Sometimes an investment adviser can be told something by a client and fail to comprehend its importance to that investor. A good illustration of this sits on the wall of one of the authors. It is a framed 500,000 Reichsmark note, which was issued by the German central bank in 1923 during the period of hyperinflation that destroyed much of the private wealth of German families. It was a gift from an investor whose family decided to implement an equity-oriented strategy for their new foundation, going against the strong advice that it should have a significant anchor of fixed income. The accompanying note read: "You simply do not understand the perils of inflation."

This book has been written against the background of a surge in rates of inflation across the world in the early 2020s after a period of around four decades of mostly declining inflation. This surge is a marked departure from the trend of the first two decades of this century, which saw steady declines in inflation (see Table 5.1). It signals not just a pickup in inflation but a pickup in concern among investors about the threats posed to them by inflation.

In Chapter 3, we discussed the corrosive impact of seemingly modest inflation on fixed retirement incomes, with 3% annual inflation almost halving the purchasing power of a fixed income over 20 years. If sustained, the pickup in inflation in 2020–22 threatens much worse damage.

TABLE 5.1 **20-year average consumer price inflation**
% per year

	1960–80	1980–2000	2000–2020
Germany	3.8	2.4	1.4
UK	8.8	4.8	2.7
US	5.3	3.8	2.1

Sources: Bloomberg; German Federal Statistical Office; UK Office for National Statistics; US Bureau of Labour Statistics

A feature of this book's approach to investment is that risk-taking should be anchored around allocations to the risk-free assets of cash and Treasury bonds. This is a core tenet of portfolio theory and traditional finance (see Chapter 4). It also reflects the practice in financial markets of pricing corporate bonds and a host of other investments every day. These financial instruments are routinely priced as a spread, that is a yield or interest rate premium over risk free government assets. But these risk-free assets are very vulnerable to inflation and for many investors the corrosive impact of inflation is one of their most important investment risks.

In the 15 years before the covid-19 pandemic, interest rates collapsed. This boosted the returns earned by investors as capital values were lifted by the decline in interest rates. In effect, the good returns enjoyed during the years of declining interest rates represented investment performance that was borrowed from the future. This has made the task of earning a positive investment return for cautious investors much more challenging in the 2020s than it was in previous decades.

In 2006, short-term interest rates in the United States and the UK were about 5%; in Germany they were about 3%, and in Japan they were already at zero. Three years later at the depth of the 2007–9 financial crisis, these rates were cut to around 0% in the United States and Europe. For a while, bond markets in each region expected this to be a temporary response to a major recession and that after a few years rates would return to more usual levels.

This did not happen. Despite the increases in inflation and, to a lesser extent, interest rates, in mid-2022, financial markets still implied that the normal range of interest rates in the United States, Germany and the UK would be anchored at levels around 1–4%. In other words, the post-pandemic surge in inflation would be seen to be a temporary blip and that inflation through to the middle of this century would normally be around 2–3.5%. This range is also broadly consistent with the targets set by the central banks, but much lower than inflation in 2022. Financial market expectations imply that current higher inflation rates are, among other things, due to temporary disruptions in the supply of food and energy.

Looking at a longer-term historical perspective gives a different reading.

History gives at best an unclear guide to the normal level of interest rates and inflation. Figure 5.1 shows Treasury yields for the United States from 1871 and for the UK from 1700. It emphasises that the second half of the 20th century, with its high and variable inflation and interest rates, was the anomalous historical period. In recent decades, economists (and financial markets) have been trying to gauge where future rates of inflation and interest would normally lie. With the benefit of hindsight, we can now see that too much attention was paid to whichever short history happened to be readily available at the time the projections were made. All three authors would admit to having thought, in the past, that 4% seemed to be a reasonable normal level of Treasury yields.

One of the biggest challenges facing investors is that no one knows where government bond yields and inflation will normally

FIGURE 5.1 **UK and US Treasury yields** 1700–2022

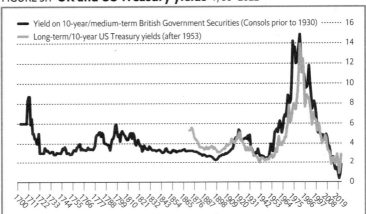

Sources: Bank of England, *A millennium of macroeconomic data*, as updated;
Robert Shiller, *Irrational Exuberance*, as updated, www.econ.yale.edu; Bloomberg
Updated to July 2022

be found in the years ahead. This also means that no one really knows the fair price for a Treasury bond either now or in the future. Figure 5.1 suggests that it would be a good thing if more advisers admitted how little they know.

Risk-free investments that are guaranteed to lose money

In the years after 2008, low interest rates savaged the income that private clients had historically received from the significant share of their wealth that they hold as cash (see Chapter 6). At the time of writing, financial markets anticipate interest income recovering a bit, but not much.

The fall in interest income removed a dependable performance cushion from cautious investment portfolios and has made lower risk investment strategies more prone to negative returns. Negative returns have a particular importance for investors, a fact that owes more to the behavioural biases and loss aversion discussed in Chapter 2 than to the simplified but coherent models of financial economics discussed in Chapter 6.

When Treasury bills offered a 4% yield, a cautious portfolio delivering 2% return would be a disappointingly modest performance. When Treasury bills offered zero, if the same cautious portfolio registered a 2% loss of value, an unmoveable benchmark would have been crossed: the same 2% underperformance became a 2% loss of capital. The building blocks of portfolio construction (see Chapter 6) are anchored around taking measured risk away from the use of creditworthy government bonds. This conflicts with the well documented behavioural characteristic of loss aversion, by which we feel losses much more keenly than gains.

The years after 2009 witnessed negative interest rates in the euro zone and Japan. In August 2019 around one half of indexes of global government bonds offered negative yields. By early 2022 this anomaly had almost disappeared.

A safe-harbour investment suggests security and reassurance that wealth or income will be protected. It seems bizarre that a safe harbour could have guaranteed a loss if government bonds were held to maturity. It seems even stranger that such investments could have been the cornerstone of a prudent investment strategy.

This anxiety about guaranteed losses from risk-free investments may prove to have been a temporary indicator of extraordinary times. But it did highlight some important lessons for investors. In particular, the decline in interest rates in recent decades made it much more expensive to secure a stable income. When long- and short-term interest rates declined from 4% to zero (which over a number of years, they did), the cost of guaranteeing a stable income for 30 years would have increased by almost 75%. In the circumstances, it is unsurprising that cost of providing pensions in the years after 2008 greatly increased.

Where, if anywhere, will interest rates be tethered?

The majority view among academics is that global shifts in demography and savings explain patterns of real interest rates and also facilitated very low inflation.[1] A single explanation seems unlikely fully to explain the declines over the 40 years to 2020 in both the real interest rate and inflation. Nevertheless, they need to be considered together. Despite a higher burst of inflation in the early 2020s, there has been intense debate among economists about whether inflation and interest rates will stay anchored around low levels (normally below 3%). This debate has focused on two separate issues.

The first relates to the apparent decline in the level of the equilibrium or natural rate of interest, over the past four decades. This is the rate of interest, *after inflation*, which is expected to prevail when the economy is operating at its full sustainable level. Latest estimates for this by economists are for a rate of interest of around 0.5% after inflation. This is noticeably lower than estimates for the turn of the century. This decline in real rates of interest around the world is normally attributed to an increase in global saving. In turn, this is often related to major demographic changes.

An alternative explanation for low interest rates is proposed by other economists (a minority) who have argued that the relentless pursuit of very low interest rates by central banks has subsidised credit and encouraged inefficiency by supporting businesses which would otherwise have failed.[2] This, they argue, has weakened productivity growth and helps to explain the low estimates of the potential growth of the economy.

It is noteworthy, given these explanations, that the demographic factors putting downward pressure on inflation now seem to be unravelling. An apparent global abundance of willing and motivated young and productive labour is being replaced by global scarcity. In the words of Goodhart and Pradhan, a "great demographic reversal" is occurring, hastened by the combined impact of two trends.

First, the accumulated impact of China's decades-long one-child policy (which has now been rescinded) has starved China of young employees. Second, the number of elderly as a proportion of those employed (the dependency ratio) is increasing in China, and also in advanced countries. For the first time in half a century the world is confronted with a tighter global labour market and this is likely, over time, to reverse the steady downward pressure on real incomes for most employees. Goodhart and Pradhan argue that this would also rekindle inflation and lift interest rates around the world.

Investors need to know that leading economists have differing perspectives on these issues. The outcome is of great importance, particularly for the living standards of cautious long-term investors who need to decide how, at what cost and to what extent, to protect themselves against the possibility that inflation will be higher than generally expected.

For example, in 2022 a cautious pensioner who had secured their income for the year by leaving it as cash would have seen an erosion in the purchasing power of that pension savings of more than 5%, almost wherever they are based. For longer time periods, the balance between interest rates and inflation looks more balanced, so long as inflation does not again exceed expectations. The plausible ranges for the prices of essential goods, or more broadly, the cost of living, in, say, 20 years' time, is one of the greatest uncertainties facing retirees (see Chapter 3).

An expectation that interest rates will remain anchored around historically low levels has led many advisers to conclude that investors need to take more risk to have a good chance of meeting their reasonable lifestyle expectations. The corollary of low interest rates normally being less than 4% for example, would imply, on many metrics, the persistence of unusually expensive stock markets. But the environment can still rapidly change. We will only know with the benefit of hindsight whether cyclical fluctuations in inflation and interest rates are now tethered to historically low levels.

Safe-harbour investments

Years of relaxed monetary policy, and uncertainty about inflation and low interest rates have encouraged recommendations for alternative ways of taking risk and of constructing investment strategies. These often include alternatives to government bonds to provide the supposedly safe-harbour component of investment strategies. In this quest, gold has always had its supporters whereas digital currencies are the new kids on the block.

Gold: a risk asset for most but an unusual safe harbour for others

Gold has been sought after as a store of value and wealth for individuals and nations since time immemorial, seemingly with some justification. Claude Erb and Campbell Harvey, professors of finance at Duke University, have calculated that, when converted into ounces of gold, the annual pay of a Roman legionary and of a Roman centurion 2,000 years ago were broadly comparable to those of a private and a captain in today's US army. Nevertheless, there can be no confidence that reliance on gold will provide a safe harbour to shelter against a storm during the lifetimes of retirees.

Gold is highly prized because it is a scarce metal which, since the earliest times, has been fashioned into the most beautiful jewellery and works of art. It helps that it is malleable and divisible, that it is readily portable, that it does not deteriorate, and that it is easy to store. These characteristics have also ensured that, around the world and through history, gold has been minted into high-value coins and used as a medium of exchange or money. The market for gold bullion is also highly liquid.

Gold has always had its advocates among investors. And increases in the price of gold so far this century, as well as financial innovation, have encouraged much wider interest in gold as an investment. Yet, despite the millennia of track record in preserving wealth, and the practical endorsement by most of the world's leading central banks, the appropriate place for gold, if any, in an investment strategy remains deeply controversial.

Economists like to be able to compare a market price of an investment with assessments of the economic value suggested by their models. This is not possible for gold. Valuation models assume that an asset generates a profit or income. For example, payments of rent give value to a property. Likewise, the earnings that accrue to the owner of a business or the interest payments made to holders of a bond give value to an equity or a bond. Corresponding calculations provide a basis for estimating the future return that might be expected from these mainstream investments. However, in the words of the World Gold Council, an industry lobby, "Gold does not conform to most of the common valuation frameworks used for stocks or bonds."

Valuing gold is probably even more difficult than valuing a work of art (see Chapter 12). Art collectors buy art because they expect to enjoy their collection. This aesthetic or psychic dividend is one explanation of the price paid for them. Gold jewellery would be comparable, and although the mythical King Midas did seem to get psychic pleasure from owning lumps of gold, bullion is different. Gold has industrial uses that could assist traditional valuations, but these uses are modest, representing less than 10% of the 3,500 tonnes mined each year.

Economic modelling is made even more difficult as this modest industrial demand for gold is dwarfed by the 35,000 tonnes, with a market value of around $2 trillion, held by central banks as part of their foreign exchange reserves. According to World Gold Council estimates, these modern stores of gold bullion represent around 20% of all the gold ever mined. They provide a modern echo of the gold treasures sealed in the tombs of the Egyptian pharaohs to facilitate their journey through eternity (though the pharaohs chose gold in the form of beautiful artefacts rather than lumps of bullion). In principle, in needy times, these vast central bank reserves of ingots of gold, which always overhang the market, could be offered for sale.

Economists struggle to explain why the price of gold is what it is and not anything else. Willem Buiter, former chief economist of Citibank and a gold sceptic, wrote in 2014 that "to a fair approximation, gold has no intrinsic value".[3]

For others this misses the point. Kenneth Rogoff, Thomas D. Cabot Professor of Public Policy at Harvard University, wrote in 2016 that "gold is valuable, because society needs to have a currency, and gold has proven an attractive option for a very long time".[4] For much of history, the relevant question was not the price of gold, but the value of everything else in terms of gold. To this day in some parts of the world, wedding dowries and gifts for religious festivals may be assessed as a weight of gold. Until the second world war, the gold standard had an important role in rigidly anchoring currencies and economies to each other through a fixed rate of exchange with gold.[5]

Since the liberalisation of the gold market in 1971, the price of gold has risen from the previously controlled price of $35 per ounce and briefly reached $2,000 per ounce in August 2020 and again in March 2022. Central bank gold holdings have been dominated for decades by the United States and European nations. Any central bank that in the late 20th century had no gold reserves and wished to diversify its holdings of foreign currency reserves will have been impressed by the gains in value that have accrued to the small number of leading central banks in the last five decades.

So far this century, a desire to diversify foreign exchange reserves away from the dollar and the euro has led to persistent purchases of gold by some other central banks. Central bank purchases and sales always have the capacity to reinforce or undermine investors who see gold as a store of value. For three decades after 1980, a period of notable weakness in the gold price, central banks were net sellers of gold bullion.

Since late in the last century, constraints on the capacity of gold mines have coincided with a transformation of living standards and personal wealth in the traditional markets for gold jewellery in Asia and the Middle East. Retail demand has been reinforced by new, more direct means to acquire gold, including gold bars and coins. This has been compounded by volatile flows into the innovation since early this century of gold backed exchange traded funds (ETFs). At the end of June 2022, these held 3,800 tonnes of bullion, with a market value of over $222 billion.

Central bank intentions remain an unpredictable threat overhanging the gold market. One of the political attractions of holding a nation's reserves in gold bullion, stretching back at least to the French president Charles de Gaulle in the 1960s, is that it gives political independence from other countries. It also offers ready liquidity and anonymity. US and euro zone Treasury bills or bonds do not give the same control and sense of independence to the owner.

Professor Rogoff compares the attractions of gold as a store of wealth with digital currencies and large denomination banknotes.[6] For many (presumably most) individuals the ability to hide wealth from the authorities is not a motivating factor. As he says, very large denomination banknotes are not needed for legitimate business and digital currencies do not have an established track record and seem unlikely to be accepted as units of value.

An owner of gold may be confident that it will have value in the future and may be encouraged by the growth of demand for gold jewellery from the rising number of wealthy families around the world. Throughout history, like Midas, many have found comfort from directly owning it. At times of breakdown in civil order, physical gold has provided a safe harbour of last resort. But it will never provide even an approximate assurance that it will retain its original value. It will always be a risk asset.

We are unable to find compelling arguments that would justify having gold as a core holding in individual investor strategies.

Cryptocurrencies: for investors, a volatile but brilliant route to nowhere?

We are similarly unconvinced that private digital or cryptocurrencies should be treated as an investment. This is not to detract from the brilliance of the original design for operating rules for a cryptocurrency, bitcoin.

Bitcoin is a dispersed, secure peer-to-peer alternative to the centralised clearing house arrangements that match both sides of transactions in modern securities markets. Modern versions of digital or cryptocurrencies trace their origin to a highly original article published in 2008, apparently by a programmer called Satoshi Nakamoto.[7] That article set out the operating rules for bitcoin, the pioneer digital currency, including the use of blockchain, a digital ledger technology. Blockchain (whose origins predate the Nakamoto paper) seems likely to pave the way for radical transformation of custody and record keeping registers in finance and beyond. Meanwhile central bank digital currencies may, over time, introduce blockchain technology into everyday money.

An early academic analysis of bitcoin described it as a virtual currency, created by programmers, which is supplied, in declining amounts, according to a known formula which simulates a limited resource.[8] Its value derives from the trust of its users and the cryptography which secures and authenticates its use.

One much-touted advantage to any owner (so long as the coding is robust) is its finite supply. Unlike central bank money, it cannot be devalued by the authorities printing more. Until the ceiling on bitcoin supply is reached, the system's design incentivises "miners" to generate a few more bitcoin to verify existing transactions. This process is incredibly energy intensive and undermines suggestions that it is environmentally friendly. Meanwhile, the broader crypto market may undermine the effect of the limited supply of particular cryptocurrencies: successful digital currencies attract competitors. The supply of each might be finite, but their supply in aggregate is not. In any marketplace, a better and more competitive mouse trap may soon arrive to threaten today's market leaders.

Digital currencies are intended to be a medium of exchange and a new form of computerised money, though they fall short on both counts. Despite this, according to CoinMarketCap, a digital currency website, the market value of over 11,000 separate digital currencies in late March 2022 was an eyewatering $2.1 trillion, similar to the value of central bank holdings of gold bullion. Its volatility was shown when this had declined by more than half in the following three months.

The supply of a digital currency may be limited, but that does not mean that its value will necessarily rise, particularly as its intrinsic use is restricted. Like gold, conventional investment analysis does not readily apply to digital currencies. There are no clear sources of expected return, no earnings from a business; no rent from a property and no contractual interest payments from a bond to anchor their value. Their prices are essentially rudderless, and so best seen as speculative investments for those who think that they will find a greater fool to sell to at a higher price at a later date before a wave of momentum evaporates.

However, there are plenty of individuals and investment firms who see profit, as well as thrill, in riding the flow of momentum while it lasts, even though cryptocurrencies are largely unregulated. Retail investors are unlikely to be supported if their investment sours or collapses for reasons the investor either discounted or did not consider.

Stable coins

An interesting subset of digital or crypto assets are "stable coins". Stable coins are intended to provide a gateway to transact easily with other crypto assets. According to the Bank for International Settlements (BIS, a club of the world's central banks), "stable coins are cryptocurrencies that aim to maintain a stable value relative to traditional currencies, such as the US dollar".

Yet stable coins are often far from stable.[9] In principle, they might be thought similar to a money-market fund, which is commonly regarded as the safest of mutual funds. But stable coins have not been regulated and the assets backing them often lack transparency and can include other crypto assets and significant **leverage**. In May 2022, one of the leading stable coins collapsed.

Despite the absence of a robust investment rationale, the rise of cryptocurrencies is leading to a wave of technological innovation and business disruption in banking and payments systems.

If payments between counterparties can be matched both automatically and inexpensively, there is likely to be transformational change in how banks, card payment companies and central banks operate in the decades ahead. This, however, seems most likely to emerge through the sponsorship of central banks and away from the crypto universe. In the words of the head of research at the BIS, "everything that can be done with crypto can be done better with central bank money – except, perhaps, for money laundering and ransomware attacks". But inexpensive and secure payments systems do not themselves constitute a meaningful investment, even though they may change how we manage our personal finances.

Altogether more interesting for investors than investing in crypto assets are the investment opportunities that may be offered by the fintech companies that are bringing crypto-related innovation, including blockchain, to banking and finance. Chapter 10 highlights this as an area of focus by **venture capital** investors. Chapter 12 looks at the new role of blockchain technology in providing a digital ledger to record ownership history (provenance) of works of art.

Cryptocurrencies attract much media comment as an interesting and challenging new group of financial instruments. They are sometimes suggested as a component of an alternative safe harbour.

Their short track record so far suggests they are, instead, unreliable risk assets that should not be expected to do well when other markets are in crisis. In such times, government bonds, whose value is supported by taxpayers and credible central banks, remain by far the most dependable guardians of value and ready liquidity.

Booms and busts

You will not be able to avoid the surprising bad times in the years ahead so you should know how you and your savings will cope with them

The notion of different market climates and the recurrence of crises is best illustrated by the fluctuations of stock market volatility over the years. Figure 5.2 shows the leading indicator and measure of stock market volatility, VIX, from 1990 to mid-2022. It gives a measure of fluctuations in the overall stock market: the higher the index, the greater the chances of large losses (or gains) in equity portfolios.

Over the three decades from 1990, the average value of VIX was 20, also approximately the same value as the volatility (annualised standard deviation of returns) reported for the longest time series of over 120 years for the US or UK stock markets.

Figure 5.2 highlights the extraordinary and temporary increases in stock market volatility during the global pandemic shock in early 2020 and in the global financial crisis of 2007–9. Investors who are sensitive to the risk of losing money might conclude that they should sell equities and reinvest in the safe harbour of government bonds or cash when market volatility increases. This is not easy. A sudden increase in volatility is likely to have been associated with a sharp fall in equity prices, making such a response a reaction to recent losses, which may prove to be temporary.

Figure 5.2 might conceal the fact that it is usual for the stock market to appear tranquil for years. Figure 5.3 shows the same data for a shorter period.

The decade before 2020 and, from an earlier period, the years preceding 2008 were largely tranquil times in stock markets, which

FIGURE 5.2 **VIX indicator of US stock market volatility**

January 1990 to June 2022

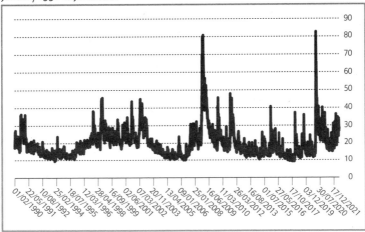

FIGURE 5.3 **VIX indicator of US stock market volatility**

December 2012 to June 2022

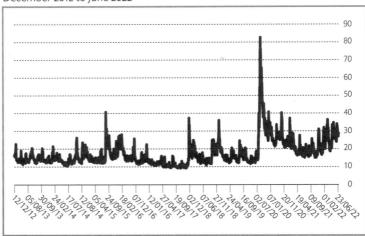

delivered generous returns, and VIX was typically well below its long-run average of 20 most of the time. In such times, it is easy for investors to lower their guard against the risk of substantial loss. Politicians can exacerbate this and join in the complacency when the good times lead them to talk of "no more boom and bust" as if wise government had abolished the business cycle.

These comfortable periods in markets can be relatively long periods in any one person's lifetime. This is when the reality of historical risks seems increasingly distant. Most of the time, the stock market is not especially volatile, but from time to time it goes off the scale. These are times of maximum danger. Short memories (especially for self-advised investors), the incentive for advisers to earn a bonus and the length of time between crises can all lead to inappropriate risk-taking.

Manias, panics and crashes

Stock market bubbles and manias happen, and some of the most readable accounts of financial markets tell the tales of extraordinary excess and subsequent collapse and personal ruin. From the comfort of hindsight, it is easy to ask: why didn't they see it coming? If something rises so much so fast, surely the subsequent fall was a disaster waiting to happen? Unfortunately, the future is rarely so clear, and rapid increases in prices are not necessarily followed by a collapse.

For over 200 years it has been conventional wisdom to describe bubbles and crises as if they are a hardy perennial of markets whose excesses reflect "the madness of people". The modern classic of this genre is Charles Kindleberger's *Manias, Panics and Crashes*, first published in 1978 and updated to include accounts of the rich vein of more recent excesses by Robert Aliber, emeritus professor of international economics and finance at the University of Chicago, and the former central banker Robert McCauley.[10]

> *What happens, basically, is that some event changes the economic
> outlook. New opportunities for profit are seized, and overdone, in
> ways so closely resembling irrationality as to constitute a mania.*

But it is always difficult to assess how much stock prices
should change when new technologies are introduced. In 2000,
Robert Shiller described a speculative bubble as "a situation in
which temporarily high prices are sustained largely by investors'
enthusiasm rather than by consistent estimation of real value".[11]

Other economists take a different approach and dislike any talk
of speculative bubbles. Their starting point is to look for rational
explanations for changes in market prices. Often the plausible
range of enhanced earnings flowing from a major innovation will
be substantial and the impact on the share prices of individual firms
that might be impacted will be large and volatile. High hopes may be
dashed and a stock price might collapse.

A classic investment error is to identify correctly the next big
transformational change, and then to think that all firms in that
sector will profit greatly from the new technology. History suggests
that few succeed dramatically, while many prove to be also rans.
The scope for investment mistakes in such an environment is large.
Many economists would say that that it is not helpful to describe a
rapid price increase followed by a precipitous decline as a bubble.
One academic study of large sudden increases in stock markets
found that "the chances that a market gave back its gains following
a doubling in value are about 10%. In simple terms, bubbles are
booms that went bad. Not all booms are bad."[12]

In a more recent history of booms and busts, William Quinn
and John Turner of Queen's University, Belfast, have likened
speculative bubbles to a fire.[13] The *spark* that ignites the fire might
be a transformative technological innovation or it might be a
government policy that is seen as underwriting private profits. The
spark is needed to light the fire, but, on its own, that's not enough; a
fire also needs fuel, oxygen and heat.

The *fuel* for a financial bubble is the easy availability of money and credit; Quinn and Turner suggest that bubbles are much more likely to occur when the yield on traditionally safe assets is unusually low. This encourages investors to "reach for yield" to meet what they might see as their reasonable income objectives. They quote Walter Bagehot, the 19th-century editor of *The Economist*, saying, "John Bull can stand a great deal, but he cannot stand two per cent. Instead of that dreadful event, they invest their careful savings in something impossible."

The *oxygen* for a bubble is marketability: the easier it is to buy and sell an asset, the easier it is to encourage a bubble. Buying an individual share is much easier than buying a whole business, and with online trading, buying and selling securities has been made easier than ever before.

The third necessary ingredient, corresponding to *heat*, is speculation. There are always investors who buy in the expectation of a quick return.

The analogy with a fire provides Quinn and Turner with an analytical framework for examining financial bubbles without being diverted by whether a movement in prices is rational or excessive.

The spark is provided, for example, by technological innovation. The fuel is provided by easy money. The scene is then set for widespread greed and wishful thinking by many investors who readily buy into an investment story which they find plausible, and which already seems validated by recent increases in prices. Such speculation by amateurs has often been propelled by professional momentum traders who look for opportunities to ride a trend in price changes, whatever its source. When these come together with rising prices, these ingredients let speculation rip and a bubble inflates.

Bubbles always end and deflate spectacularly. A three-year-old would ask "Why?" One answer is that if the buoyant price level did not deflate at least quite rapidly, it evidently was not a bubble – because that is what bubbles do. Or, in the words of former chairman of the US Federal Reserve Board, Alan Greenspan, it is because it is "very difficult to definitively identify a bubble until after the fact – that is, when its bursting confirmed its existence".

It is easy to say how investors should respond if they see what seems to be speculative excess in a market. They should make sure they know how much of their wealth is exposed to the apparent excess, and, mindful of the possibility that their analysis might be at fault, they should ensure that their ultimate goals are not threatened by that exposure. It's important to differentiate between a seemingly expensive market which would naturally accompany unusually low government bond yields, and an expensive market which seems to reflect over-optimistic earnings projections and investor euphoria. The former might lead to prolonged high market prices, whereas the latter could be undermined in an instant.

Apparent excesses are unlikely to affect the entirety of a well-diversified investor's wealth, although, in any subsequent correction, multiple markets are likely to be affected. Long-term investors, with a balanced approach to risk-taking and a healthy degree of scepticism of their ability to time markets, are unlikely to make more than marginal changes to their investment strategy.

Do markets overreact?

The argument that markets overreact and then revert towards trend or even overshoot in the opposite direction is closely related to the arguments in favour of a value style of equity investing (see Chapter 8). In brief, it recommends buying when cheap and selling when dear. Such arguments also apply to the level of the stock market. As ever, our message, drawing on years of experience, is that it is easier said than done.

Robert Shiller made considerable use of his indicator, the cyclically adjusted **price/earnings ratio**, also known as CAPE, or the Shiller PE,[14] in his book *Irrational Exuberance*, the publication of which in early 2000 coincided with the peak valuation of the US market. His measure shows a pronounced pattern of stock market overreaction and reversion towards the mean. He showed that for well over a century, high levels of the Shiller PE have tended to be followed by relatively poor stock market performance, and low levels of the Shiller PE by better than average performance.

With hindsight, few would dispute the importance of the message this gives at extremes of valuation, and this emphasises the benefits of being able to adjust strategy. However (and there is usually a however), Shiller would acknowledge that it is unclear how far the persistence of lower interest rates in recent decades should be expected to have raised stock market values. He has also shown adjustments which suggest that the high CAPE ratio does not look out of line with the unusually low bond yields after 2012. In short, if government bonds are expensive, it should be no surprise that equities are expensive.

The equity market is not alone in appearing to show some tendency for valuations to revert towards trend. Corporate bond yields provide another indicator of value that seems to range between periods of offering only a modest reward for risk-taking (as immediately before 2008) and periods of offering the prospect of generous risk-adjusted returns. This is discussed further in Chapter 9.

Avoiding speculative excess is easier said than done. In practice, success does not come easily even to professional investment managers who seek to time markets. The perils of this were highlighted by the sudden and dramatic decline in equity markets around the world in February and March 2020 as large parts of the global economy were shut down by governments in response to the covid-19 global health pandemic.

In the United States, this marked the end of the longest bull market in the S&P 500 index of leading US companies since inception of the index in 1926. The index declined by 34% in 33 days, even more precipitous than in 2008 when the index registered a larger cumulative fall of 46% but over 200 days. In March 2020, the Fed (and other central banks) came to the rescue (see Chapter 7) and reversed what then became the shortest bear market (often defined as a decline from previous peak levels of more than 20%) since 1929.

Other than as a generic risk, the pandemic, with its indirect severe and sudden impact on financial markets, was unexpected. Other setbacks in global markets (for example, the deflating of the 1980s boom in the Japanese stock market in 1989–91; the global financial crisis of 2007–8; and the technology, media and telecom share-price declines of 2000–2) typically echoed the warnings of at least some experts.

The pandemic highlights the need to doubt one's ability to anticipate market setbacks, and always to have an investment strategy that meets immediate and longer-term requirements, even if the market environment should suddenly change. This sense of modesty encourages some to argue that long-term investors should stay close to their strategic asset allocations (see Chapter 6) and buy and hold equities and bonds through thick and thin.

Self-advised investors need to be especially aware that their investment conviction, even if well founded, may take a very long time to be validated. Even long-term investment funds such as university endowments or **sovereign wealth funds**, which may be confident of enduring from generation to generation, can find it difficult to act as truly long-term investors.

This difficulty of institutional investors behaving as long-term investors offers a salutary lesson to individuals. For an institution, the mundane necessity of maintaining the confidence of a fund's stakeholders matters throughout the investment journey. Investment policies that are prospectively rewarding but, in recent years, underperforming, may easily lead to a reversal in policy, which, with hindsight, might be judged ill-timed. To paraphrase a supposed aphorism from Keynes, markets can stay irrational longer than institutional investors will tolerate an underperforming investment committee.

If an individual investor uses an adviser, the success of the relationship will depend on many things (see Chapter 2). Often, the role of luck will be underestimated. There are no rule books to help investors distinguish between an adviser's well-justified tenacity and the same adviser's stubborn refusal to recognise that markets have changed and a different policy is needed.

To weather these uncertainties and risks, long experience suggests that it is better to be a tortoise than a hare, and to stick to a steady programme of adding contributions to a sensible strategy. Booms and busts, good times and bad, will influence how we feel along the way, but it is safest to assume that we will not be able to avoid the crises in markets and inflation that will occur in the years ahead. The next chapter discusses how investment models can help investors cope with these challenges.

Will model allocations help me invest better?

Simple model allocations are easy to explain and help all investors stay disciplined. They are widely used

Model allocations between stocks, bonds and cash are commonly used by investment advisers to represent different grades of risk-taking. These allocations typically divide investments between safe-harbour and risk assets, with cautious strategies having a higher policy allocation to safe-harbour investments. Portfolios can also vary in terms of liquidity to make it easier for investors to change strategy if and when their circumstances change. An important feature is that model portfolios anchor actual investments around the model allocations, no matter what is happening in markets.

Whether investors should stay close to a fixed allocation between cash, equities, bonds and other investments is deeply controversial. Twenty years ago, the late Peter Bernstein, an influential adviser, wrote that "investment in today's environment should be opportunistic, to be played more by ear than by rigid policy allocations". He went on to quote Keynes, who wrote 100 years ago, "The long run is a misleading guide to current affairs. In the long run we are all dead. Economists set themselves too easy, too useless a task if in the tempestuous seasons they can only tell us that when the storm is long past, the ocean will be flat."

As we've seen, whether investors should be able to profit by timing their exposure to the stock market is largely a debate between those who think that the pattern of stock market performance is a statistical random walk, and those who think it predictably follows cycles of lean times and plenty. For the former, forecasting is pointless but, on average, risk-taking is rewarded. The latter believe that market returns are mean reverting, with booms or higher than average returns being predictably followed by busts or periods of disappointing returns. This debate has important implications for investors' allocations between stocks, bonds, cash and other asset classes.

Formal model portfolios (sometimes called policy portfolios) are widespread. They are used by investment firms which advise large numbers of private investors; by corporate pension plans, university endowments and sovereign wealth funds, the largest investment funds in the world. By acting as benchmarks, these model allocations help to anchor and monitor the management of investments, often within pre-agreed limits. They help to express an attitude to risk-taking even though we know that market volatility and the risk of loss fluctuates between benign periods of relative calm and episodes of manic disruption (see Chapter 5). Self-advised private investors should consider whether such a model allocation would help to anchor and provide structure to their investments, or whether they would prefer to follow Bernstein and play it more by ear. A combined nine decades of working with almost every type of investor persuades us that we ignore model allocations at our peril; they are a useful discipline for any investor.

One of the great insights of modern portfolio theory, which can be used to design model portfolios, is the *portfolio separation theorem* of the late James Tobin, a Nobel prize-winning US economist. Tobin suggested that the degree of investor risk aversion influences the allocation of an investment strategy only between the two poles of risky and cautious investments. As the economist Willem Buiter wrote in 2003, in an appreciation of Tobin's contribution to economics:

This is an important and beautiful result, which is not done justice by Tobin's own summary: "Don't put all your eggs in one

basket." Indeed, Tobin's remarkable result is better summarised
as "regardless of your degree of risk aversion and caution, you will
only need two baskets for all your eggs".

Investment advisers repeatedly lose sight of this essential principle. They frequently think they have discovered new and improved ways of diversifying investment portfolios which falsely offer the benefits of security at higher rates of return. As we discussed in Chapter 5, one dilemma facing investors so far in the 21st century is how to benefit from Tobin's insight while allowing for the lower rates of interest paid on high-quality government debt.

Tobin set out his theorem in 1958.[1] He explained how investors with different attitudes to risk choose to allocate financial investments in varying proportions between cash and volatile assets. Although Tobin's theorem seems overly simplistic, it is a useful reference point and, in practice, widely used by investors. The theorem, which is also known as the mutual fund separation theorem, relies on strong assumptions (see below). If we are willing to make these, then using an investor's degree of risk aversion to allocate investments between risk-free and risk assets will provide a suitable strategy for any investor. This is, in effect, common practice among investment advisers. However, the underlying assumptions present challenging obstacles. They include that the global market for risky investments is fully represented by listed equities (which it is not); that the prices of risky investments are determined efficiently (which they are not); that expected returns in excess of the risk-free rate are constant (which they are not); and that an investor's degree of risk aversion follows textbook economics, which is unlikely (see Chapter 2's discussion of loss aversion). So what are the implications for investors?

In practice, to address the shortcomings of this highly simplified approach requires high-fee, actively managed investment strategies, whereas Tobin's two-investment approach can be proxied by low-cost global equities and cash (or government bonds). The costs of the more complicated versions, which seek to address the criticisms of Tobin's simplified model, place them at a significant disadvantage to the simplicity of the low-cost, two-portfolio approach. The simplified allocation between diversified equities and cash or government bonds remains a useful reference strategy for investors, and, in effect, reflects practice for many financial advisers and a benchmark model portfolio for many institutional investors.

The role of anchoring is particularly important in model portfolios: an investment adviser may have thought that safe-harbour government bonds were undesirably expensive and may have recommended moving quite a long way from the allocation and **duration** of the benchmark allocation into other assets. These different investments will have introduced new risks but, if the adviser's forecast was correct, they should reduce the exposure of a capital loss being incurred on expensive bonds.

The model portfolio provides a benchmark against which to measure that decision. It also provides an anchor to drag investments back towards the model if the pricing anomaly subsequently corrects. Policy asset allocation helps to keep investments in line with a previously agreed approach. They give a framework to judge deviations from that agreed approach and sometimes to anchor moves by advisers from that policy in pursuit of tactical opportunities. Cautious advisers choose to stay quite close to the investment strategy implications of Tobin's insight.

Government bonds or Treasury bills also provide an important anchor for model allocations designed for investors with different risk tolerances. The weight given to them is driven by the appetite for risk of the investor. Risk assets are represented by allocations to equities. Whether equities alone represent the most efficient way of gaining access to premium returns needs to be assessed in the light of market valuations and expectations for performance, risk and diversification from different asset classes at a particular time. It will be normal to invest in a range of risk assets including, for example, credit and real estate.

These opportunities are discussed in later chapters. But no

matter what an adviser believes about the predictability of market returns or which asset class is cheap or dear, a cautious investor will be keener on having safe-harbour assets than an aggressive investor.

Risk-taking and portfolio rebalancing

As we saw in Chapter 5, at times of market turmoil, measures of volatility increase and the value of risk assets falls. Any investor who has benchmark allocations to risk assets and conservative assets will then be underweight risk assets; in other words, they are likely to have less than their benchmark allocation to risk assets because they have fallen in value. Correspondingly they will be overweight safe assets.

In these circumstances, investment advisers – who, as we've seen, may enjoy taking risk more than their clients do – often recommend rebalancing towards model or benchmark allocations. This is likely to involve selling government bonds (which may have risen in price) and reinvesting the proceeds in risk assets, especially equities (which have declined in price). This counter-cyclical policy is not for the faint-hearted. It provides liquidity to distressed sellers and increases risk-taking in bad times when risk premiums may be unusually high. But if markets tend to overreact and mean revert, this added risk-taking will be a source of added value.

Automatic rebalancing, either on a fixed time schedule or when differences from benchmark allocations exceed an agreed threshold, is a natural strategy for a long-term investor. It's a way of taking more risk when others wish to take less as market volatility increases. It is also a way for investors to anchor policy to a previously agreed strategy justified with reference to past long-term averages for market risks, which are unlikely to reflect the circumstances at the time of the rebalancing.

Focus on the short term or the longer term?

Model **asset allocations** sometimes distinguish between long-term and short-term investors. We believe they always should.

Short-term investors have a clear focus on **total return** as a measure of the success of their investment strategy. They are "absolute return" investors, for whom the safe-harbour investment strategy is to be 100% invested in cash, as they may need to spend their wealth in the near future.

An overriding desire to keep things simple may encourage many whose spending plans are better described as long term (because their wealth is needed to fund longer term spending) to focus on the same measure. This can be an expensive mistake. Instead, long-term investors should focus on whether their wealth is sufficient to support their future commitments, like a pension.

We've already seen the difficulty of staying with a long-term strategy when short-term performance is disappointing. A particular danger is that long-term investors who focus on absolute returns will miss two important differences between short-term and long-term investing. The first is the focus that long-term investors must have on price level and inflation uncertainty. The second is the failure to distinguish between a reduction in the price of future security (a fall in government bond prices and a rise in Treasury yields) and a reduction in the market's assessment of an investment's quality.

Declines in prices are sometimes good for you

Sometimes you can be sure that a financial loss can be reversed. Pensioners living off the income generated from a well-constructed portfolio of high-quality government bonds can respond to a fall in the market value of these investments with composure. It will reflect an increase in government bond yields and *if the increase in yields reflects strength in the economy rather than higher inflation*, it should be of no concern. It will keep them in the style to which they are accustomed.

Higher interest rates (and lower government bond prices) reduce the cost of buying future income. This is unambiguously good news for anyone saving to provide income for tomorrow. Higher interest rates mean both lower bond prices and being able to meet more of tomorrow's needs with each new regular investment.

However, individuals who suffer a similar fall in investment value because of a downgrade in the creditworthiness of a corporate or a credit fund should feel less comfortable. They might reasonably suffer sleepless nights, because there is less assurance that they will get paid.

Some might say that it is not the credit downgrade that should concern the investor, as it is only a default that leads to a loss of income. But this is a classic case of the dangers of mismeasuring risk. Investors lose sleep over their ability to support their future standard of living a long time before most downgraded corporate bonds default.

For a short-term investor who may wish to sell the bond in the near term, either reversal could lead to a permanent loss.

To achieve success as a long-term investor, this distinction between good and bad price declines should be accepted and reflected in how an investor responds to financial reverses. This is important advice for investors who often regard any loss as if it is bad news, even though, when interest rates rise, it may represent an opportunity to lock in access to higher future income.

How safe is cash?

The anchor investment for short-term investors is cash. Cautious investors who want more security should hold more of it, and many investors hold a lot of it. International investors (for instance, ex-pats temporarily living abroad or families living in several countries) need to decide what counts as cash and in what currency, or combinations of currencies. Such combinations, probably reflecting the spending and residency plans of the investors, may change over time, complicating measurements of value, investment performance and risk-taking.

Allocations to cash are often represented in model or example investment strategies as if they are always invested in risk-free Treasury bills. This is rarely the case. One of the most shocking features of the 2007–8 credit crunch's early stages was the sudden erosion of confidence in cash investments held at banks and in **money market funds** (widely seen as one of the easiest and best ways to invest cash).[2] This was coupled with uncertainty about the attitude of governments to bank failures and the extent of government deposit insurance. It was a ripe environment for crowd behaviour by savers as they responded to rumours of impending bank failures.

Concerns about the security of bank deposits were allayed by the clarification of deposit guarantee schemes, and by the growing understanding shortly after September 2008 that deposits at major banks would be protected, not least by the steps taken to bolster bank capital. It remains the case that unguaranteed cash investments in banks need careful due diligence and money managers respond to this by offering liquidity and money market funds to manage these risks. With low interest rates and the need to pay fees to the managers, the yields on these funds are typically modest, and when they are not, investors should seek an explanation.

Do bonds provide insurance for investors?

The answer is sometimes yes and sometimes no. The normal pattern is that when equities do well, bonds tend to do at least quite well. In other words, equity markets and bond markets are positively correlated with each other. At times of crisis and flight to quality, however, this relationship often reverses as investors flee to government bonds.

During the initial phase of 2020's pandemic crisis, global stock markets declined sharply and the excess of yields on corporate bonds over government bonds (**credit spreads**) widened, giving disappointing credit performance. So, credit typically did poorly as the stock markets fell. Long-term government bonds, by contrast, after some hiccups, appreciated, and provided welcome diversification to investors.

In the United States, Germany and the UK, among other creditworthy countries, government bonds diversify best when diversification and liquidity are most needed, that is, in bad times. Decades of investment experience tell us that this is one of the most dependable lessons of financial market history.

But the scale of the insurance payout depends critically on the size of the allocation to government bonds, the initial level of yields on bonds and the duration of those Treasury securities. At other more distant times in the past, against a background of creeping increases in inflation, equities performed quite well while bonds disappointed, being eroded by inflation and suffering a gradual increase in yields.

So in times of crisis government bonds normally appreciate, but not necessarily by much (even for longer maturities), and not by as much as equities fall. Seeing bonds as an insurance sometimes works but not always.

The other lesson is that the relationship between different maturities of bonds is generally predictable, with the longest-dated (and most volatile) US Treasuries appreciating most in periods of stock market crisis. But this does not always happen. When it does not, the shape of the bond yield curve (see Chapter 4) can shift markedly. This argues for investment in a range of bond maturities. Long-dated bonds are unquestionably much further away from a short-term investor's safety zone than short-term bonds and so are much riskier. But the payout of short-term bonds is much less when fixed-income markets are providing insurance.

So the process for short-term investors should be first to decide how much risk they want to take, and then to make sure that the risk-taking is itself diversified across asset classes. Offset equity exposure with at least some fixed-income exposure, not, in this case, for income, but for insurance. But do so knowing that this is one of those insurance policies with loopholes in the small print.

"Keep-it-simple" long-term asset allocation models

"Diversify, diversify", asset allocators often say. However, in designing low-risk strategies, which should always be the starting point for asset allocation, the first step should be to design the best very cautious strategy to neutralise (or hedge) the risks of failing to meet objectives.

For some investors, Tobin's portfolio separation theorem suggests that this could, conceivably, be achieved through a single holding in a particular creditworthy government bond. Diversification becomes an issue as an investor moves away from this best hedge. Any such move needs to be made efficiently, which will call for the diversification of avoidable risks.

So, what does a long-term investment plan look like, and how should it be structured? It is not a wealth plan – rather it is a long-term income or spending power plan. An income plan needs to take account of your financial and other assets, your likely earnings, your financial obligations and your spending aspirations. As discussed in Chapter 3, the first step for those planning for retirement, for example, should be to check the income you could buy from an insurance company either linked to inflation or as a fixed annual monetary amount. This will probably be disappointingly small, but it will establish a base case to see if there is a minimum-risk annuity available to hedge out or secure retirement plans.

Even a cautiously managed long-term strategy involves a significant risk of falling short of financial objectives. However, for most private investors, there is no fixed pattern of cashflows that need to be targeted. A financial plan that incorporates flexibility (as well as investment risk) to respond to changing investor needs or aspirations provides advantages that should be compared with the expensive, inflexible attractions of guaranteed government or insurance company pension payments provided by, for example, annuities.

Should long-term investors hold more equities?

Chapter 5 discussed stock market bubbles and the debate among academics and investors as to whether stock market risk evens out the longer you stay invested in the stock market.

Even if investors doubt their ability to time markets, if booms and busts in the stock market predictably follow each other, it may be possible to profit from this pattern. The prevailing view is that the predictably cyclical nature of equity returns reinforces the case for a somewhat higher allocation to equities for long-term investors.

Various studies, notably by Jeremy Siegel, Russell E. Palmer Professor of Finance at the Wharton School of the University of Pennsylvania, have suggested that over long holding periods (for example, 30 years or more) an investor might be more confident of the after-inflation performance from equities than from conventional government bonds.[3] Siegel's evidence comes primarily from the United States, but it also appears to be supported, almost without exception, by international data. Taken together, these would suggest that skewing the investment strategy allocation for long-term investors towards equities and away from bonds is sensible, for cautious as well as aggressive investors.

Inflation: always eroding living standards

There is no role for cash in long-term models. This is because cash, though stable, is volatile relative to government bonds which are the better safe harbour for long-term investors. It also normally offers no performance advantage. Despite this, we know that private investors from around the world still keep significant allocations to cash (see later in this chapter).

As a minimum requirement, views on expected inflation and the margins of error in these opinions should be reviewed from time to time. Simple what-if illustrations for the price level at different dates in the future, rather than just average inflation rates, can help. Where nominal income will be fixed, this can provide a ready reckoner for standard of living uncertainty in the decades ahead. A key decision will be the extent to which the holdings of government bonds should be in the form of inflation-linked or conventional bonds, and then how much should be exposed to private credit.

The chance of a bad outcome may be higher than you think

A cautious short-term investor will be less tolerant of short-term losses than an aggressive investor. But what is a bad outcome or minimum acceptable return (MAR)?

For cautious individual short-term investors, an adviser might, for example, suggest that they should have an investment strategy that has a risk of losing no more than 5% in a year. It is likely that such a strategy is reckoned (by the adviser) to have no more than a 1 in 20 risk of experiencing an annual return worse than −5%. This would be the target MAR and refers to the perceived chance of an outcome worse than the specified parameter in a particular year.

The MAR might be assumed to be −10% for moderate risk investors, and −15% for aggressive short-term investors. In principle, any figure could be selected. Whichever figure is chosen, the likelihood of suffering a performance worse than the suggested tolerance limit is likely to be much greater than the investor might reasonably expect.

First, it is likely that the probability is calculated for an individual calendar year. However, over five years, for example, the probability of breaching the guideline in at least one of these five years will be more than one in five. If, as is most probable, a portfolio is monitored more frequently than once a year, say at the end of each month, the probability of at least one breach, measured based on rolling 12-month periods, will be closer to 50%. These things happen and are not surprising, even if you or your adviser think that a 1 in 20 risk is remote.

Having selected appropriate tolerances for losses, an adviser (who may be a robo-adviser – see Chapter 1) can, in theory, use these guidelines to consider model strategies that give the best prospect for wealth generation. They are the efficient portfolios that are optimal for each indicated level of risk-taking by investors. Efficient portfolios give the best possible trade-off between expected risk and expected return. For any given level of risk-taking there is, in theory, only one optimal portfolio. It would be impossible to achieve higher expected returns with no increase in risk and it would be inefficient to pursue the same returns, but at higher risk. In practice, because we cannot model uncertainty, even though we may expect that a particular outcome is unlikely, we generally do not know with any precision how unlikely that result is.

A consequence of this is that these indicated MAR risk figures can support a range of very different strategies, and the intention would often be to manage the strategy to a lower level of risk-taking than indicated by the MAR.

Consider the three illustrative short-term strategies, using only stocks, bonds and cash, shown in Table 6.1, which have stylised allocations to global equities increasing from 20% to 50% and then to 75%. The allocation of non-equity investments is divided between US Treasury bonds and cash.

Data supporting the moderate strategy could, for example, indicate that a return of −8.3%, or worse, should be expected with no more than a 1 in 20 chance in any particular year. The back-testing of results using monthly data over a quarter of a century shows that much larger negative returns would have been recorded in the past with such a moderate strategy. In the 12 months to February 2009,

TABLE 6.1 **Model short-term investment strategies, with only stocks, bonds and cash**
as percentages of total assets

Asset allocation	Unaggressive strategy	Moderate strategy	Aggressive strategy
Equities	20	50	75
Government bonds	20	50	25
Cash	60	0	0
Total	100	100	100

Source: Authors' illustrations

at the depths of the financial crisis markets would have delivered a negative return of 22%.

This illustrates that experience can from time to time be much worse than would be suggested by the past average statistics for overall returns and volatility. The more comforting figures for apparent risk-taking are provided by routinely used modelling exercises. These suffer from severe averaging difficulties which suggest, for example, that stock market volatility stays at one average level. It does not, and (as 2008 and March 2020 demonstrated) the worst returns are experienced when this is least true.

The risk figures are undermined by the surprising frequency of extreme returns – by trending or momentum in markets, and by the fact that, at times of stress, past average relationships between different markets probably won't hold.

As an example, consider the yield curve (Chapter 4), which is usually upward sloping: ten-year yields tend to be higher than three-year yields. A particular vulnerability is when short- and long-term interest rates move in different directions (in the jargon, if the yield curve becomes inverted).

This can happen, for example, if the Federal Reserve or other central banks are seen to get serious about inflation worries by raising short-term interest rates and thereby causing medium-term inflation worries to abate. Short rates would rise but longer rates might ease. This can disrupt financial markets if hedge funds and other investors have borrowed short to fund lending long. Often though, the market environment is benign, returns are positive but not euphoric, a comfortable air of complacency surrounds investors, and lax risk-taking is encouraged.

Is your low-risk strategy providing insurance to someone else?

There is another more specific reason why seemingly low-risk, normally low-volatility strategies may fail to provide the expected degree of protection in bad times. Many low-volatility investments indirectly offer insurance to someone else and are in effect option-writing strategies, which collect a steady insurance premium but then occasionally suffer surprisingly large losses.

This does not just affect some hedge-fund strategies (see Chapters 4 and 10). Less obviously, corporate bonds also fall into this category (see Chapter 9). Providing this insurance becomes more of a liability to investors as equity volatility increases, so we should not be surprised that corporate bonds, as a group, perform particularly poorly when stock market volatility increases.

Cautious investment strategies, which reach beyond government bonds to the more attractive yields on offer from corporate bonds, normally perform as expected with a decent yield and low volatility. But in bad times, as was seen in the 2007–9 financial crisis and in March 2020, they can perform particularly poorly. Typically, no hint of this intrinsic risk exposure will be evident from marketing track records and risk statistics for such cautious strategies if they only reflect performance during tranquil markets.

Families and wealth

Individual investors often have inflexible spending habits. They may expect that they can ride out short-term losses because they take comfort from the large increase in investment values in recent decades. These seemingly comfortable levels of wealth reinforce their own belief that they are long-term investors. A particular source of wealth illusion is that investors do not grasp how lower interest rates necessitate a substantially increased accumulated wealth to support a particular lifestyle. This illusion is exacerbated if investors (or advisers) come to see the unsustainable investment returns of the last four decades as if they are normal. They are not. Such investors (and advisers) can easily make the mistake of thinking they have sufficient assets to support an incautiously high standard of living. They might get away with it, but there is a significant risk that they will not.

There is often little predictability in the spending plans of individual family members. Sometimes there are clear dates associated with particular financial goals that could easily be benchmarked using government bonds. In other cases, wealth is explicitly needed for opportunities (or contingencies) that may arise in the short term.

This creates wealth-planning issues that do not affect other investors. With families, strategic objectives and actual disbursement of wealth can evolve at short notice, sometimes in surprising directions. This brings uncertainty into the time horizon for the management of private wealth, which has few parallels for institutional investors. It also helps to explain private clients' large holdings of readily available cash, so that they can more easily respond to new spending demands or opportunities.

Changing strategy: an unavoidable risk

Whatever strategy is being followed, from time to time it is likely that investors will be persuaded that they need to change investment direction. The process of changing strategy can be fraught with risk. There is often little advice available on how to decide when to change strategy. But, for all investors this can be a crucial issue.

Implementing strategy change involves making an unavoidable judgment about market timing. This must be balanced against the knowledge that your investment risk profile is not what you want it to be – presumably why you want to change strategy in the first place.

A simple rule to follow is that, if investors decide that their risk profile is too aggressive, they should move promptly to the new, more cautious strategy. Such investors should not let seeming confidence in short-term market forecasts extend the period during which their risk profile is inappropriate. However, for all investors, within each four- or five-year period there is a significant chance that circumstances may force a change of direction. Larger allocations to illiquid investments always complicate this process. Adjustments to strategy involve taking views on markets and costs and, typically, a significant degree of regret risk (see Chapter 2).

The real issue is not that market timing in liquid markets cannot be undertaken skillfully or profitably: it can. There are some investment managers whose skill in market timing has manifested itself over time. But these track records are not built by one-off "bet the ranch" decisions on the timing of corrections to inappropriate risk profiles. They are carefully managed and, within limits, diversified. Changing strategy is different. There is normally no way to diversify the investment decision or to give meaningful time to profit from the correction of perceived market anomalies.

It is often suggested that phasing implementation of a change in investment strategy from one asset class to another is the best way to proceed if an investor wants to change tack. Large investors often implement change this way to reduce the impact of their changed strategy on market prices. Other investors are also likely to feel more comfortable with this approach. But the strong argument in favour of immediate implementation of change is that, if an investor has decided that the risk of the current investment strategy is excessive, any delay extends unnecessary risk-taking. When faced with the need to make such a decision, there are always reasons why now is not the best time to act.

How do other investors invest?

Any investor likes to know how their investment strategy compares with others. This harks back to Chapter 2 and the role of anchoring in how we take decisions and how we get comfortable with the reasonableness of whatever we decide to do. Everyone's circumstances are different, but everyone likes to cross-check their allocations and recommendations with those of other investors.

Surveys exist showing the average asset allocation of different groups of individual and institutional investors from different regions of the world. Individual investor investments typically exclude their family home (but not second homes). Despite this, surveys show a higher allocation to real estate investments by individual investors when compared with institutional investors such as pension funds.

Why do private investors hold so much cash?

A particular feature of Table 6.2 is that it shows (as do other surveys) that private clients typically have large allocations to cash and liquidity, allocations that some see as inefficient. Consultants might see high cash holdings as contrary to their model of how private investors ought to invest, and conclude that investors are being wasteful. A more plausible explanation may be that the model used by these advisers is wrong.

The willingness of private investors to hold a significant proportion of their wealth in low-yielding liquid investments might reflect an undisciplined, relaxed approach to their management. But more importantly, it reflects their flexibility in investment objectives and spending intentions. A buffer of cash gives investors the option (which is intrinsically valuable) to respond to changed spending plans and opportunities which often arise at short notice.

TABLE 6.2 **The pattern of asset allocation by global high net worth private investors**
as percentages of total assets

	Equities	Fixed income	Real estate*	Alternative investments†	Cash & equivalents
Jan-18	31	16	17	9	27
Jan-22	29	18	15	14	24

*Real estate excludes primary residences
†Alternative investments include commodities, currencies, private equity, hedge funds, structured products and digital assets
Source: *Capgemini World Wealth Report 2022.* "High net worth" refers to individuals with financial wealth of at least US$1m, excluding primary residence, collectibles, consumables and consumer durables.

Investors are comforted by the assurance given by the ability to drawdown cash reserves in bad times, when, in the words of Antti Ilmanen, a dollar of ready cash feels especially valuable.

In practice, the broad patterns of asset allocation have evolved but not changed markedly for different groups of investors in the years since 2007, despite the marked changes in inflation and government bond yields. The changes that are evident are often continuations of trends that were present even before the global financial crisis. Whether consciously or not, most institutional and private investors responded to the appreciation of stock markets and the historic reductions in bond yields as if they were not sure how to interpret indications that markets were expensive.

Most investors will spend much more time focusing on the detail of implementation, which involves departures from this keep-it-simple approach. Surely the FAANG stocks, Microsoft and Tesla are much too expensive? Why do I own so much Taiwan Semiconductor? What about old economy value stocks, and aren't emerging markets inexpensive? Is high yield too risky? Why do I have so much in international equities? Am I invested in the most suitable real estate investment trusts?

Despite the time that most investors spend on these issues, the most important one is the extent to which the investment strategy plausibly secures the investor's spending plans and whether that seems appropriate for the investor's appetite for uncertainty and risk. The keep-it-simple framework is more than adequate to help focus on these issues.

What is often thought to be the more exciting material about the different asset classes is covered in the remaining chapters of this book. When reviewing these more alluring and sophisticated opportunities, key questions to keep asking are: How will this investment perform? Would I need to sell it? And would I be able to sell it at a reasonable price in bad times when reliable diversification will be most important to me and my need for cash may be greatest?

Liquidity risk: in bad times, cash is king

Maintain a buffer of cash. We don't know
when bad times will arrive

Most investors probably consider themselves to have the capacity and temperament to be **contrarian** investors, to hold their nerves and stick to an agreed sensible strategy when markets turn sour. We often delude ourselves, although the ample cash holdings of many private investors should allow an unhurried response when markets turn sour.

In early 2020, the unfolding covid-19 pandemic led governments around the world to impose lockdowns on their countries and economies. In response to the lockdowns, equity markets declined precipitously and corporate credit markets froze. Within weeks, stock markets had rebounded and credit markets thawed (though more slowly) as central banks provided them with unprecedented support.

These few weeks were a time when investors were exposed to the risk of lasting damage, either through rushed decision-making, or because a lack of ready cash forced them to realise investments at greatly disadvantageous terms. It was a time when investors who needed to sell, sold what they could rather than what they wanted. The early months of 2020, together with the more extended global financial crisis of 2007–9, provide a stark reminder that liquidity, the ability to draw on cash or sell investments at close to its current price, is a key dimension of risk-taking.

The decisive intervention by central banks in debt markets in recent crises might encourage investors to assume that a floor will normally be provided by the authorities under any credit crunch. That would be a dangerous assumption, especially if an investor knows that they need regularly to sell assets or that they may need to raise more cash in bad times.

An ample buffer of liquidity – an investment portfolio that has a good proportion of liquid assets – is the best first line of defence against liquidity crises in securities markets. This gives investors time to take stock and to reflect. Almost always, the investors who suffer most in sudden liquidity crises are those who lack ready liquidity, especially if their investments have been funded by debt or bought "on margin", which is the same thing.

As we've seen, keep-it-simple strategies, anchored around holdings of creditworthy government bonds, should be liquid as well as simple. These strategies provide benchmarks for individual investors. Actual investments will differ. Government bonds, for example, might need to be replaced in large part by corporate bonds or private credit (see Chapters 9 and 10). Inevitably, the strategy is likely to become more complicated and as it does, the strategy usually starts to embrace more liquidity risk.

Although illiquid, infrequently valued private market assets are said by some to be more attractive because infrequent pricing makes them seem less volatile (see Chapter 10). This is a dangerous and misleading conclusion, which has probably been encouraged by the responses of central banks to the liquidity crises of 2007–9 and 2020, when many heavily indebted companies, both private (and, therefore, not routinely valued by the market) and others listed on the stock exchange, were kept afloat thanks to the easy and cheap availability of liquidity in large parts of the global economy.

A century ago, Keynes said this about the risk of **private investments**, where valuation is always at best an estimate:

> *Bursars will buy without a tremor unquoted and unmarketable investments in real estate which, if they had a selling quotation for*

> *immediate cash available at each audit, would turn their hair grey.*
> *The fact that you do not know how much its ready money quotation*
> *fluctuates does not, as is commonly supposed, make an investment*
> *a safe one.*[1]

But, as shown by the example of the pricing of UK open-ended property funds, also known as property unit trusts (see the box), this lack of instantly updated market prices is still, 100 years later, often seen as an attractive feature of illiquid investments. In an echo of the warning from Keynes, Clifford Asness, a hedge fund manager, has warned that "many investors may come to rue their addiction to the phoney smoothness" of the performance of private investments. Keynes went on to say, "it is safer to be a speculator than an investor" in the sense that "a speculator is one who runs risks of which he is aware and an investor is one who runs risks of which he is unaware".[2]

Some very British liquidity crises: open-ended property fund suspensions in 2008, 2016 and 2020

Making the same mistake time and again might be thought a peculiar sort of madness. Few investment funds had to suspend sales by investors of holdings in their funds during the sudden market crises of early 2020, but prominent among these were UK open-ended property funds, which offer daily or weekly liquidity to investors to buy or sell at surveyors' valuations.

This group of funds also suspended redemptions due to material uncertainty in market values during the global financial crisis of 2008–10 and also following the unexpected result of the UK's Brexit referendum in 2016.

German regulators responded to the impact of the global financial crisis on domestic property funds by introducing minimum holding periods of two years and notice periods of 12 months. An exception was made for legacy retail investors who wished to make modest sales. Elsewhere, and in particular in the United States, Australia and Canada, the normal route for individual investors to access managed (rather than directly owned) property investments is to invest in one or more real estate investment trusts (REITs).

A REIT is a stock-exchange-listed vehicle where potential imbalances between purchases and sales are brought into balance through immediate price changes. The pricing mechanism for the UK's remaining open-ended property funds is clunky by comparison. REIT prices are normally much more volatile than property fund prices, because REITs automatically put a price on investors' demand for liquidity. In bad times, this is always expensive.

In responding to a 2021 regulatory review of pricing problems with the UK's open-ended property funds, one comment was that REITs did not offer an appropriate substitute due to their price volatility. This argument is specious. The difference between the administered values of open-ended property funds and REITS during a liquidity crisis gives a measure of the price that investors in real estate are willing to pay for liquidity and immediacy. UK property fund managers responded that the lockdown crisis introduced material uncertainty into fund values which led them, once again, to suspend transactions.

REITs, with their market prices to bring balance between supply and demand, traded throughout.[3]

Illiquid investments are not suitable for short-term investors. In addition, illiquidity restricts an investor's flexibility, and so should not be countenanced unless there is confidence in superior returns or better diversification.

Performance in private markets is strongly influenced by the skill of managers, the extent of leverage that the managers use to amplify their returns (also for good or ill) and the level of fees that they charge.

These are markets where salesmen boast of their fund's superior past performance, but where, unlike investments in stocks and bonds, investors cannot presume that they will be able to perform even averagely well. In liquid equity and bond markets, any investor can have confidence in being able to earn the market return (for good or ill) at modest cost by investing in an index fund, which mirrors the performance of the entire market. This does not apply to private markets.

The key to unlocking returns in private markets is information, and accessing this requires payment of high fees. Investors have to believe that their managers have skills that enable them to deliver at least market returns. Investing in an arrangement that lacks this edge will incur premium costs, add inflexibility and condemn the strategy to inferior performance.

Liquidity is a dimension of risk which is not captured by the off-the-shelf risk models that are routinely used in managing investments. This is because it is difficult to model, not because it does not matter. For long periods when markets are benign, this may not seem to matter. But it does.

One problem with illiquidity is the difficulty in defining it. One definition might be the proportion of the current price you need to give up to sell the asset immediately. Another definition might be the time it takes to sell an asset without dropping its price. In addition to time and price, there is a third dimension to liquidity risk – quantity.

Quantity matters when considering the impact on the share price of the sale of a significant proportion of a company's shares. Individual investors may think this may matter for large funds but not for them. But an individual investor may easily have a small investment in what is likely to be a large fund, and that fund may have a dominant shareholding in a small company. If the fund is unable to sell this holding, except at a punishing discount, each individual investor in that fund will be hurt by its illiquidity.

Investing in illiquid markets

If the first heresy of investing in illiquid investments is to think that infrequent pricing somehow makes them less risky, a second heresy is to think that because an investment is illiquid, it always offers a premium return. This can be an expensive mistake. There is no automatic illiquidity premium.

The appropriate way to appraise an illiquid investment opportunity is to see if it offers the prospect of generating a premium return. If it does, it needs to be sufficient to compensate adequately for giving up the flexibility offered by liquidity. Inconveniently, an investor's own demand for liquidity can be surprisingly high when markets are least willing to supply it. Given a cautious assessment of the investor's circumstances, and after allowing for fees, an illiquid investment opportunity will often not pass the suitability test.

This gives rise to two related questions.

- How should investors judge their appetite for illiquidity (in other words, the trade-off between the potential to earn excess returns in return for accepting the near certainty of added inflexibility that comes with illiquidity)?
- How should investors assess the returns to be expected from a particular illiquid investment?

Investors also need to take into account higher fees, an almost universal characteristic of investing in illiquid markets.

Andrew Ang has analysed these and other issues that arise in trying to determine an optimal allocation to illiquid investments. An immediate problem is that traditional "mean variance" optimiser models historically used to derive recommended asset allocations for investors assume that investors can rebalance their portfolios at any time. This does not apply with illiquid investments.

This inability to rebalance investment allocations imposes real opportunity costs on investors and can result in unwanted risk-taking. A particular aspect of this, which is easy to overlook, is that the ability to rebalance portfolios back to a long-term strategic allocation is a means of seeking a liquidity premium from securities markets. Investors who are heavily exposed to illiquid markets will be much less able to benefit from this.

Ang concludes that long-horizon investors do have an advantage in investing in illiquid investments. However, this does not mean that it is optimal for all long-term investors to hold them.

Liquidity budgets

One of the lessons that emerged from both the credit crunch of 2007–10 and the pandemic stock market reversal in early 2020 is that all investors need a policy on liquidity management. This became evident as investors scrambled to respond to a situation where formerly liquid markets became prohibitively expensive to trade.

The impact of this on investors' liquidity and cashflow was compounded in 2020 when previously reliable payments of equity dividends and real estate rent were quickly reduced or suspended. Against this background, the advantages for investors in having a good balance between liquid and illiquid assets are clear. All investors ought to have an explicit policy on allocations to liquid and illiquid investments and, if relying on income distributions, an understanding of how much they rely on income payments from risk assets.

Illiquidity in normally liquid markets

Liquid markets give investors the option to buy or sell an investment at a time they choose at prevailing market prices and at modest cost. Illiquid markets do not give them this option. Like any option this is valuable. The value that investors put on it varies substantially over time and between investors. Investors who particularly value liquidity will need to be offered a premium rate of return before investing in illiquid assets. Correspondingly, investors should always pay less for an illiquid investment than for an otherwise identical liquid investment.

Liquid investments should provide the **natural habitat** for short-term investors, even for aggressive short-term investors. This is because they may need to realise investments at short notice (which is why they are short-term investors). Long-term investors can more easily accommodate illiquidity and with skill (or luck) may profit from it. However, the global financial crisis of 2007–9 and, briefly, the 2020 pandemic shock, showed that some markets that are usually liquid can become illiquid surprisingly quickly. In normally liquid markets, this means investors can sometimes be forced to accept damaging prices that they would prefer to avoid.

Private investors commonly have large allocations to cash, which should make it easier to behave as patient investors. Long-term investors, however large or small, can profit from fluctuations in market liquidity, so long as they are able to use skill in drawing down their reserves of cash when others need it most, and when market prices are depressed. But, as we said in Chapter 5, this involves taking more risk when others want less risk – and so is not for the faint-hearted.

8

Risk assets: global equity markets

Investing in a global equity tracker fund can be a surprisingly sensible way to invest in equities

If adjusting your investments to reflect environmental, social and governance priorities, remember to keep your investments well diversified

In Chapter 5, we suggested that investors might need only two types of investments for their investment strategy.

■ One represents cautious investments that could be either creditworthy domestic Treasury bills or government bonds with a maturity and payment schedule suitable for the time horizon of their spending plans.

■ The other could be a well-diversified basket of risk assets, representing an expectation of better, if uncertain, performance.

As discussed in Chapter 6, a common thread of simplified versions of modern portfolio theory is a recommendation that these investments – one cautious, the other risky – should be held in a proportion appropriate for the investor's tolerance for disappointing outcomes.

Equity index funds

An index fund reflecting the entire listed global equity market is often taken as a reasonable approximation to this generic global risky investment. Individual investors with modest savings can now access such funds at a cost that much larger funds would not hesitate to pay for their more sophisticated strategies, probably with a surprisingly similar performance objective. Few of the world's largest institutional investors would regard the performance of that modest investor's benchmark easy to outperform consistently, and there will be plenty who will have fallen short of that benchmark.

Index mutual funds, which automatically buy a market weight of each stock in a stock market index, without a thought being given to quality or price, were first offered for sale in the mid-1970s.[1] And, in recent decades, there has been a spectacular growth of market-matching index-fund investing.

Index funds are a major innovation which have saved investors tens of billions of dollars in fees and costs. In previous generations, this would have been paid to active equity managers who charged high fees researching, on average with little success, to back what seemed to be the most promising companies.

Index funds give investors access to the performance of a chosen market index. So successful has been the rise of index investing that it has given rise to concerns about the accountability of index funds for the governance of the companies that they collectively own.

This will always seem remote from the concerns of individual investors, and exercise of voting rights (part of an oversight of companies known as *stewardship*) may seem an irrelevant distraction to an individual. Despite this, the exercise of ownership responsibilities by index funds is an increasingly important issue.

In the United States, just three fund management companies – Blackrock, State Street and Vanguard – dominate the market for index tracking funds. Academics have calculated that these three fund managers collectively voted around 25% of the shares in all S&P 500 companies in 2019, a proportion which some see rising to

40% by 2040. They argue that fund manager commercial incentives encourage them to underinvest in stewardship and from time to time to defer to the wishes of the managers of the companies they are holding to account.

Ultimately, this matters for individual investors and it seems likely that in the future individual investors in equity funds may have the ability to cast votes at the annual general meetings of the companies in which they indirectly have a shareholding.

In the past, larger institutional investors were sometimes criticised for behaving like absentee landlords by ignoring or reducing their shareholder responsibilities to a box-ticking exercise. Each of the managers of index-tracking funds emphasises their commitment to promoting good governance in the companies their investors indirectly own. But this is light-touch governance. It contrasts starkly with the focused responsibility and involvement with businesses typically undertaken by **private equity** managers (see Chapter 10). These governance issues are now centre stage for many, with a widespread focus on environmental, social and governance (**ESG**) issues by investors, stakeholders and also by regulators.

Index funds, "every vote counts" and who owns companies?

In 2020, 47% of US households owned mutual funds.[2] These are often index funds. The proxy votes cast by the managers of index funds at company annual general meetings (AGMs) on behalf of these millions of American investors guide the governance of US listed corporations. They are cast without consulting the ultimate owners of the funds and they are overwhelmingly set by those three fund management companies, Blackrock, State Street and Vanguard. Regulators are now focusing on this.

In March 2021, Allison Herren Lee, then acting chair of the Securities and Exchange Commission, gave a speech in which she talked of shareholder democracy and empowering investors to hold the companies they own to account.

One of the three fund managers, Blackrock, announced in late 2021 that it plans to let some investors exercise their implicit voting rights on behalf of the shares that they indirectly own through their holdings of Blackrock funds. Blackrock's CEO, Larry Fink, said that the company is "committed to a future where every investor – even individual investors – can have the option to participate in the proxy voting process if they choose". It is likely to be some years before investors in mutual funds have this flexibility.

A precondition is almost certainly large investments by fund managers in back-office technology. How far these changes will matter for how companies are managed and how they perform is unclear. In 2022, the British journalist Merryn Somerset Webb published *Share Power*, subtitled "How ordinary people can change the way that capitalism works and make money too". There is a move to encourage all investors to have the ability to vote (whether directly or by directing the manager of their funds) their shareholdings.[3] When this will be possible, whether many will choose to become involved or will, by default, become engaged through the policies of the platforms that they use, are important unknowns.

Environmental, social and governance in investing

In recent years, scientists, governments and investors have focused increasingly on the impact of business on climate change. These concerns are often grouped by investors alongside seemingly unrelated matters of corporate governance, including measures of diversity among employees and the composition of boards of directors. These fall under the catch-all heading of environmental, social and governance or simply responsible investing.

An important concern for economists is that some viable businesses would not be profitable if properly costed to take account of their impact on the environment and so on future generations. Instead, there exist what economists call "externalities" which impose costs or benefits on society. These are not reflected in market prices, but they should be if resources are to be allocated efficiently.

An uncontroversial micro-example of this could be the costs inflicted on anglers (and others) when factories discharge waste into a river which endangers the stock of fish. When the cost of cleaning up the pollution is levied on the factories, the polluters pay and the value of those companies should fall to reflect this. To some extent this already happens through regulation and taxation, as well as through pressure from shareholders and other stakeholders.

This example of the polluted river is a helpful allegory for the plight of the planet. The challenge for investors is that externalities that threaten the future of the planet are not easily costed by investors, other than by policies to sell out of companies they view as harmful. Disinvestment is a blunt instrument to encourage changes in corporate behaviour. Some large investors use disinvestment as a final step if discussion with companies does not lead to the changes in corporate management that they are seeking. Applying such pressure is not really an option for individual investors acting alone.

Some investors also adopt strategies that restrict investments in carbon-emitting sectors. Government support has facilitated economies of scale that have led to greatly increased use of clean energy, such as wind and solar while displacing use of fossil fuels. In the same vein, the EU has pioneered a market which puts a price on carbon emissions by industry, and so puts a price on the social cost to future generations of emissions by industry. The widespread focus by investors and investment managers on ESG investing shows that investors often wish to supplement, in their capacity as owners, the impact of government policy with their own ESG priorities. In Europe, regulation now requires institutional investors to account for ESG factors when making investment decisions.

Some academics have argued that the traditional focus on an investment's total return performance misses the **utility** or value that investors may place on whether their portfolio is "doing good", and whether it is avoiding firms with whatever they judge to be objectionable business practices. Some investors who wish to emphasise ESG themes in their portfolios may gain satisfaction (or utility) from a combination of doing good as well as doing well.

Others may believe, perhaps encouraged by fund salesmen, that responsible investing is a probable route to superior performance. Investors may expect that stranded assets (such as oil company petroleum reserves that may never be drawn down) will be worth less than the market expects. If so, investors who avoid such companies may expect eventually to be rewarded, an expectation backed up by surveys of individual investors in the United States.

However, the enthusiasm of these investors for ESG strategies may be short lived if the strategies are seen to underperform. There is already evidence that hedge funds have bought positions in stranded assets and established "short" positions in favoured ESG stocks that are believed to have been bid above some estimate of fundamental value. For other ESG investors it may be sufficient that they feel that they have done some good by avoiding investment in fossil fuels.

The story here is complicated by the catch-all nature of ESG and responsible investing. That investors should want companies to be well governed is common sense: research suggests that better governed firms tend to perform better than poorly governed firms. The financial impact of a focus on raising standards in environmental and social practices of listed companies is less clear.

Investors who wish to let ESG considerations influence their investments should choose an investment manager whose ESG concerns align with their own. This is likely to involve accepting a higher level of fees than investing in broad index funds.

Although the leading index providers publish indexes for the main markets which are tailored to accommodate ESG concerns, as always, the devil is in the detail. Competing providers of the ESG credentials of listed companies have shown remarkably inconsistent results: one source may list one large company as ESG friendly and another the same company as ESG unfriendly. This matters as the ESG indices are often (incorrectly) regarded by investors as substitutes for each other.

Dimson, Marsh and Staunton separately conclude that there appears to be some correlation between corporate, social responsibility scores and financial performance by companies, but it is not strong and the causation is unclear: "We cannot say whether firms that do good, do well, or that firms that do well, do good."

In a similar theme, Mark Anson and colleagues from the Common Fund, a US manager of non-profit investment portfolios, have also highlighted the biases that are typically found in investment funds that have adopted ESG criteria for investing.

These funds are typically underweight energy, utilities and industrial companies while being overweight technology and healthcare companies. In other words, they have a bias towards growth companies. These tilts in ESG portfolios seem to explain much of the performance differential of ESG mandates with the broad market rather than ESG being a reliable marker of better performance.

They were also unable to identify an underlying tendency for ESG mandates to outperform the broad market, though a bias toward some FAANG stocks such as Amazon will explain why for a period of years ESG mandates performed apparently well. In addition, the popularity of ESG strategies is likely to have led to an increase in demand and so prices of widely accepted ESG stocks. Any impact on performance from the popularity of ESG strategies is likely to have been short lived. This has nothing to do with earnings and is similar to the transient impact on performance seen when companies join or leave a widely followed stock market index.

Will ESG crowd out my style?

There is a range of different ways to fine-tune global equity exposure in an attempt to get an edge and to improve performance or diversification. Often, these opportunities to invest in different styles of equity investing are being applied alongside ESG priorities. This can lead to muddled responsibility for investment decision-taking, whether the performance outcome is disappointing or surprisingly good.

The starting point for diversified equity investing should normally be a passive exposure to the global market, which typically means buying an index fund which gives a representative exposure to every company in the global stock market. This is both inexpensive and readily available.

But a global tracker fund will not suffice for investors who wish to avoid investing in firms with what they regard as harmful business practices. Others will stay with an inexpensive global tracker fund, taking comfort from the index fund manager being able to engage with company management on their behalf as owners. Others may be sceptical of ESG concerns and regard them as a passing fad. Yet others will say that government and international regulations provide the key to correcting business activities that harm the climate.

In any event, the performance and risk characteristics of a global tracker fund help to clarify the performance consequences of deviating from the market, although the knowledge that company accounts may not properly reflect the costs inflicted on society by business suggests that this benchmark is not ideal.

The restless shape of the global equity market

At the start of the 20th century, railroad stocks represented 63% of US equity; 120 years later, that percentage was less than 1%.[4] Japanese companies accounted for 45% of the global stock market in early 1989, but by 2020 this had diminished to 7%. In 1988, emerging markets represented 1% of global equity markets but 20% of world GNP; in 2021 emerging markets accounted for 11% of global equities and 44% of the global economy.

The scale of these changes should be a powerful challenge to anyone suggesting that investors should passively accept whatever changes may occur in the stock market. It is valuable to pause from time to time to consider whether one or other markets or industries is substantially under-represented or overvalued.

Despite the extraordinary changes in the shape of the global equity market, an annually rebalanced, passive approach to investing in US, UK, or global equities, had it been available, could have performed extremely well over the past 12 decades (see Chapter 4). In future, investors can now easily replicate this through a low-cost global index fund.

However, the belief that it should be possible to do better than to match the performance of the stock market seems to be supported by the well-documented existence of a wide range of persistent anomalies in returns for groups of stocks. Simple arithmetic, however, tells us that this cannot be true for all stock market investors. An important area of debate is whether the apparent stock market anomalies that have delivered better risk-adjusted performance over time are best seen as rewards for taking different types of additional risk rather than pricing anomalies.

Over the years there has been extensive analysis of these well-established patterns of stock market performance that do not conform with the predictions of the original simplified theory called the *capital asset pricing model (CAPM)*. In its original form, the CAPM said that the performance of any stock reflects two things:

- the extent to which its share price tends to rise or fall with the market (known as its **beta**)

- a considerable amount of company-specific volatility.

The first represents a stock's exposure to **systematic risk** for which investors should expect to be compensated, because it cannot be diversified away in an equity portfolio. An example of a stock that would be a "geared play" on the stock market, or a high-beta stock, would be the stock of an equity money manager whose fee income, reflecting assets under management, would rise and fall in line with the stock market and whose profitability would be geared to this influence.

The second is **noise**, or idiosyncratic or diversifiable risk. This should cancel out in a well-diversified portfolio, but it reflects the scope for an individual stock, or a portfolio of stocks, to perform differently from the market (or, more precisely, from the beta-adjusted market return).

There have been many refinements to the CAPM to reflect research indicating that there are different sources of risk that can help to explain share **price performance** relative to the market as a whole. These include interest-rate and foreign exchange exposure, and also data on corporate balance sheets, including market capitalisation, income and dividend history, industry and geographical location. An understanding of these sources of risk helps investors put together equity portfolios with exposures that they expect to be well rewarded.

The division of portfolio risk into undiversifiable, systematic market risk and diversifiable, idiosyncratic risk is the fundamental insight of the CAPM. It has stood the test of time. It gives an invaluable framework for understanding how an investment manager changes the performance and risk of a portfolio. An understanding of this insight, as well as an appreciation of its strengths and weaknesses, is an important aspect of the interface between finance theory and practical investment.

Underdiversification of equity investments

Underdiversification is the ugly name given by academics to the difference between an investor's equity investments and the composition of the global equity market. It is an indication of avoidable risk-taking and is a source of inefficiency, except where investors can expect to benefit from those differences.

In personal investments, underdiversification often reflects behavioural biases as much as deliberate investment decisions. This includes overweighting popular growth stocks with lottery-like characteristics, and meme stocks, driven by social media fan clubs, technology funds and even employer stocks. For investors, an important message from Chapter 4 is that concentrated equity portfolios will normally underperform the stock market: it is not a 50:50 chance, even before allowing for transaction costs and manager fees.

Underdiversification is much wider than this.[5] It is also reflected in a tendency, seen around the world, and in both institutional and private investments, to allocate more to home-country investments than would be suggested by their country's weight in the global market. Although this is less pronounced than a generation ago, it is still pervasive. This is called the home equity bias. However, some tilt towards domestic equity investments may nevertheless be called for.

Home bias: how much international?

In recent years, investors around the world have allocated a growing proportion of their equity investments to international markets. They often do this inefficiently. When investors diversify abroad, they typically start with markets that are geographically close and not those that are unconnected or, in the jargon, least correlated. The less connected or correlated two companies are, the better their shareholdings; when held together, they will smooth each other's volatility and diversify each other.

The reasons for the home equity bias have been debated widely. For decades a tenet of finance theory has been that global diversification helps to reduce risk with no impact on expected return. Hence the multitude of research papers that have tried to explain why investor portfolios routinely deviate from this simplified theoretical recommendation. Possible explanations include whether investors show a better understanding of risks, such as exchange rate risk, and potentially inferior cash flow matching by overseas investments. These are ignored by the simple model. Other explanations include behavioural biases which lead to inefficiencies and excessive risk-taking.

International investments and currency hedging

For investors with a clear home currency, investing in foreign equities and bonds involves foreign currency exposure. This should not be a problem so long as it is appropriately assessed and, if need be, managed. For some low-volatility investments, introducing currency risk is likely to overwhelm whatever rationale existed to make the investment, unless the currency exposure can be **hedged** away (see below). For high-volatility investments, such as equities, the investments will be volatile whether or not they are hedged. This issue is more complicated for the many tens of thousands and their families who work abroad and who may have earnings and spending plans in more than one currency.

An intuitive explanation of currency hedging

Currency risk is a manageable risk. It is also a big risk that, incorrectly handled, can lead to windfall losses (or gains) of 20% or more over a 12-month period. Currency hedging is the way to manage this risk in international investments.

The intuitive way of understanding currency hedging is to remember that it is equivalent to placing cash on deposit in the investor's home currency (for example, US dollars) and borrowing the equivalent amount in a foreign currency (for example, euros). This would hedge an investment by an American in continental Europe. In this way, fluctuations in the exchange rate will wash out, having an equal and opposite effect on the foreign investment and the foreign debt. The investor's investment return will then be the performance of the foreign investment in foreign currency (euros), plus the interest rate on the domestic currency deposit (US dollars), less the interest rate on the foreign currency debt (euros).

The more conventional way to describe this is to say that foreign currency risk can be neutralised through foreign exchange hedging, where an investor contracts to sell foreign currency at a date in the future (or "forward") at the current exchange rate. The contract allows for differences in interest rates between the two countries. Typically, the contracts are for one or three months. They are then rolled forward and adjusted as needed to reflect any changes in value of the underlying investment. This makes sure that any capital appreciation (or decline) remains fully hedged.

What does currency hedging achieve?

Currency hedging manages currency risk and, for many investments, provides a marked reduction in the volatility of international investments. This is most clear in higher quality or **investment grade** bonds (see Chapter 7). A marked reduction in volatility is clear when high-quality foreign currency bonds are hedged for currency risk.

By contrast, currency exposure in international equities adds little to the volatility of equity investing. A common rule of thumb that follows is that international investments in bonds should be hedged but that international investments in equities do not need to be hedged. With hindsight it will sometimes have been profitable to have hedged equities and at others to have been unprofitable, but either way, the investments in equities will have been volatile.

Research has shown that this generalisation about hedging international equities may need qualifying to allow for the tendency for safe-harbour currencies to strengthen at times of equity market weakness (and vice versa).[6] The original research was published in 2010 and covered the period before the global financial crisis. It suggested that investors from safe-harbour countries (notably the United States) would have fared much better at times of crisis if their international equity investments had been hedged. The corollary of this is that investors with a **base currency** that weakened at times of crisis suffered smaller losses if they left their international investments **unhedged**.

At times of crisis, there is a cash flow asymmetry between

stock market losses and losses on foreign exchange contracts. Foreign exchange contract losses have to be made good with cash immediately; investors can reflect on stock market declines at leisure (when market fortunes may reverse). In bad times, when cash is likely to be at premium, losses on foreign exchange contracts can be very painful. There is no rule that says that the US dollar will always appreciate in a stock market crisis (rewarding an American's currency hedged international equity fund) or that the British pound will always weaken (rewarding a UK-based unhedged international equity fund).

This asymmetry between cash gains and losses from hedging in bad times reinforces the case for leaving international equities unhedged unless investors believe that their home currency will be a dependable safe harbour in bad times. This may be the worst possible time for you or for the managers of your investment fund, if the fund is "hedged for currency risk" and your currency weakens. They will need to find large amounts of cash if your home currency depreciates when global stock markets are also enduring bad times.

Currency hedging has (historically, at least) given US dollar investors an element of valuable (and inexpensive) insurance that has provided a payout at times of crisis. Inexpensive insurance policies that are likely to pay out in bad times are particularly attractive to investors. But always beware the potential liquidity costs of surprisingly large adverse exchange-rate movements, and remember that the past may not be a reliable guide to the future.

Are domestic equities a better match for domestic expenses?

An argument for allocating a greater weight in strategy to domestic equities than their weight in the global equity index is that domestic equities may be a better match for domestic currency obligations than international equities. If domestic equities are a more useful investment to meet domestic expenses, then some home-country bias is warranted.

For example, home currency dividend payments are more helpful in meeting payment obligations than the volatile prices of foreign equities. However, the country in which a company lists its equity is often a poor guide to where its revenue is earned. It follows that some home bias in investment allocation to help match liabilities is theoretically appealing, but in practice researchers find this difficult to confirm or to quantify.[7] The results have generally been inconclusive. For individual investors, it seems likely that the diversification benefits of a fully global approach are likely to be sensible and appropriate.

Some of the behavioural biases discussed in Chapter 2 may also play a role in the home bias in equity allocations. For example, investors may favour markets closer to home that managers perceive that they understand better. There can also be an unspoken wish by managers to control how far their recommended strategies differ from their peer group, as well as inertia. There can be more mundane explanations. Foreign investment is often discouraged, for example, when it involves greater costs such as transaction taxes. Despite much research, no single explanation adequately explains the widespread home-country bias in equity investing.

Less discussed is a home-country bias towards home-country industries. Investors outside the United States who overweighted domestic equities will simultaneously have underweighted the technology and web-based companies that have transformed business and driven global stock markets over the last 25 years. Technology companies represented 20% of the FTSE Global All Cap index at end June 2022 but, for example, only 1.3% of the UK's FT All Share Index, 12% of the FTSE Eurozone 300 index and 28% of the FTSE US index.

UK investors with a home bias in their equity allocations will probably have underperformed relative to the global index. This is a vivid illustration of the potential cost of underdiversification. For personal investors, it seems reasonable to cut through the debate about global equity diversification by taking the shortcut to an unhedged global index fund. This is probably as good as a small investor can hope to get, and it will have served them well in the past.

The US dollar's role as a safe harbour suggests that when the possibility of hedging the currency exposure of international equities is available, that US dollar investors should take it. But there are no guarantees that this would be a profitable decision. It would still lead to drains on liquidity at any future time of dollar weakness.

Underdiversification and investment style

Underdiversification can also arise from the investment styles that are sometimes recommended by advisers and consultants (see Chapter 2). Many advisers have a view that particular themes are likely to be well rewarded in the years ahead. Our recommendation is for caution and to be aware of the extent of differences from the market opportunity that are being suggested. Apparently well-considered investment strategies led many international investors to miss much of the increase in wealth represented by the transformation of global business over recent decades.

"Small cap" and "large cap"

It has been known for more than four decades that over extended periods of time smaller companies have outperformed larger companies. This result has been confirmed on many occasions for the United States, the UK and other countries. The general pattern is that the smallest companies (micro-companies) have outperformed small companies, which in turn have outperformed large companies. This is known as the "**small cap** effect" or the "small cap anomaly", so-called because the historic outperformance is too large to be explained by the original simplified CAPM model, even though small companies tend to be more volatile than large companies.

The historical performance of small and **large cap** companies in the United States or the UK gives a measure of the small cap effect. This can be seen from a comparison of the performance of the largest US companies with that of small companies.[8] The cumulative outperformance of small cap since the data begin in 1925 is impressive, with an initial $1 investment growing (for one definition of small cap, before allowing for inflation, or expenses and taxes) to $27,500 by June 2022, compared with $5,650 for an investment in the group of largest companies. (Over the same period, consumer prices increased 15-fold.) This translates into an annualised performance of 11.2% per year for small cap stocks, compared with 9.4% for the large cap stocks (and 2.9% per year for inflation). A similar pattern is clear from research in the UK and in other countries.

This tempting track record does not offer an entirely free lunch. In the United States and the UK, small caps have still underperformed large cap stocks in over one quarter of rolling ten-year periods since the indices started. Such periods of multi-year underperformance by small stocks are sufficient to caution most investors against holding much more than a significant minority of their equity investments as strategic holdings in small cap stocks.

First, investors need to understand what is meant by small cap before they decide on allocations. Different small cap managers have different investable universes of stocks. Many money managers would regard stocks in the United States or Europe of less than $5 billion market capitalisation as small cap, with a market cap range of $5 billion–$10 billion as mid cap and anything above that as large cap. The market is dominated by a small number of mega-cap stocks, and the most valuable companies in the FTSE Global All Cap index at end June 2022 were five companies (Apple, Microsoft, Amazon, Tesla and Alphabet, the owner of Google), three of which had over $1 trillion market capitalisation. Together they represented almost 11% of global stock market value. This was roughly the weight in the global index of the next two largest country markets (Japan, with 6%, and the UK, with 4%). The United States accounted for 59%.

Second, exposure to small cap stocks should be monitored. There is a tendency for active investment managers to drift into small-company holdings, partly because they may be less well researched by competitors. Active managers may range significantly within loosely defined investment remits and passive managers may manage money against index benchmarks that do not reflect the market. Wherever possible, as a guide to potential underdiversification, seek out (or ask your adviser for) information that aggregates your underlying exposures to individual companies and then compares them with the broadest possible measure of the market.

Special purpose acquisition companies (SPACs)

SPACs are blank-cheque listed companies that have been set up as funded companies, typically sponsored by private equity companies (see Chapter 10). They usually have a limited shelf life of two years, during which time they need to find an existing private company to acquire. Otherwise, investors are returned their investment, less the heavy fees charged by the SPAC's sponsor. They offer a shortcut route to listing a private business and were particularly popular during the covid-19 pandemic of 2020–21. From an investor's perspective, they have provided a particularly risky ride that also came with payment of high fees.

Don't get carried away by your style

As we saw in Chapter 2, equity investment managers usually have distinctive investment approaches and philosophies, or investment beliefs, which lead to differences in style of investing. These characteristics are often as ingrained as any personal belief. Investors need to know and understand these differences. They will often find that some approaches are more appealing than others because of the sort of person they happen to be. Investors should be careful not to let such preferences result in unwitting risk biases in their investment strategy.

Philosophically, value and growth managers are quite different.

Value managers

Value managers believe that markets repeatedly overreact to investor enthusiasm or pessimism. They are contrarian individuals who are likely to make a virtue of implementing unfashionable investment decisions. Their approach assumes that market prices oscillate around their fair values and that the turning point, when valuations become extended, is unpredictable. They will try to persuade their clients that patience is needed, as eventually the strategy is sure to be rewarded.

Value managers tend to invest in mature companies, typically with established patterns of revenue and earnings, which seem to be selling at historically attractive prices. However, over the ten years to 2021, value stocks underperformed the broad market, which was driven by US technology companies. Many investors seem to be most attracted to value investing when a value manager has experienced recent superior performance.

A major vulnerability for value managers is changes in the structure of the economy and business. An oft-repeated aphorism is "The four most dangerous words in investing are: it's different this time." But the transformation of global business by web-based innovators in recent decades reminds us that sometimes prospects for individual industries and the rapid emergence of new companies really do make a difference.

Growth managers

A growth manager is likely to criticise value managers for looking back and not spotting potential. For growth managers, analyses of technological and commercial change, and how this can transform the earnings prospects of individual companies, industries and economies, provide the basic drivers of new investment opportunities.

Growth managers invest in companies with the prospect of rapid but uncertain growth. Such companies often do not have long track records and so an investment may be justified by how well that company is placed to profit from disruptive change in a particular market.

Recent years have provided rich pickings for successful growth managers, who are particularly concerned to profit from the relationship between earnings growth and stock price performance. Companies rarely post unusually strong earnings growth results year after year. But as the market discounts the strong earnings of those companies that are growing rapidly, their stock prices can rise very strongly. It's an investment approach that puts a premium on primary research into companies that may demonstrate unexpectedly rapid earnings growth in the future.

In contrast to growth managers, a core role for value managers is screening established databases to find companies with attractive characteristics. Many growth managers also use statistical screening of databases, but this is a much less powerful tool for growth managers than successful detailed company, industry or thematic research. But such research is notoriously difficult to undertake successfully and consistently.

Over the longest periods of time, by most measures, value stocks have normally been shown to have outperformed growth stocks. But there have been many periods of underperformance by value stocks, especially in recent decades. This underperformance of value (up to 2021) is attributed by some researchers to a failure of traditional measures of value to allow for the increasing importance in the modern economy of intangible assets, such as intellectual property. Value investors would emphasise that a prolonged period of underperformance is exactly the wrong time to lose faith in value. In turn, critics would say that a failure to pre-empt transformative changes is an enduring weakness of value investing.

Many investment managers have strong views on the superiority of their preferred approach to investing. However, strongly held and apparently well-founded views can underperform for much longer periods than most investors can easily tolerate. Campbell Harvey's warning in Chapter 4 suggests that investors should be sceptical when presented with apparently well-researched strategies to beat the market. Maintaining balance is a prerequisite to sleeping easily. Agnosticism about competing styles of investing strengthens the case for simplicity in investment arrangements.

How much in emerging markets?

Since the late 20th century, developed markets have (in aggregate) declined in weight in global equity markets as emerging markets, particularly in Asia, have grown in importance. The MSCI Emerging Markets Index represented less than 1% of the world market in 1988, a figure that had grown to only around 11% at end June 2022, with China representing 33% of the Emerging Markets Index.

It's important not to conflate emerging *markets* with emerging *economies*. Emerging markets, as classified by MSCI, include such comparatively developed economies as the Czech Republic, Israel, South Korea and the United Arab Emirates.

Opinions about the role of emerging markets in global equity portfolios differ. Some favour them because of their increasing importance in the global economy, their diversification benefits, and the hoped-for prospect of higher rates of return. Faster GDP growth in these markets has often been given as a reason for expecting superior returns, but this is controversial.

History shows that the link between a country's economic growth and the domestic equity market can be more tenuous than is often supposed. There are several reasons for this. First, much of the GDP growth can reflect the activity of the government sector, the **unlisted** private sector, or of companies listed in other countries. In addition, even in emerging markets, domestic listed companies may earn much of their profits from abroad. Dimson, Marsh and

Staunton "find no evidence of economic growth being a predictor of stock market performance".

Emerging equity markets are more volatile than developed markets. It is safest to assume that this reflects inferior diversification in emerging markets, which is not a risk that should lead to an expectation of higher returns.

Historically, it also seemed that emerging markets behaved as if they provided a leveraged (that is, exaggerated) exposure to world markets, which would lead to higher expected returns. Recent experience has been more mixed. When developed markets do well, emerging markets also do well, but not reliably better. Likewise, when developed markets suffer sudden setbacks, emerging markets typically suffer, but not predictably more than developed markets. If the performance of emerging equity markets suggested a geared or high-beta exposure to world markets, this would be a reason to expect premium returns from emerging markets, but we do not see it.

Since the MSCI index started in 1988, emerging markets have (to June 2022) outperformed developed markets in only 38% of rolling ten-year periods. This suggests that investors need to have the appetite and capacity, within their global equity exposure, to stomach the greater exposure of their allocation to emerging markets to illiquidity and to potentially disruptive changes in financial environment.

A long-term investor might take as a point of reference for their allocation to emerging markets not just the weight of these markets in the global index but also their weight in world GNP. The best guide to this is probably the World Bank's 2017 International Comparison study which estimated that the global economy (when measured using purchasing power parities rather than market exchange rates) was split almost equally between high-income and low-income economies. By far the largest of the low-income economies is China, which is roughly the same size as the United States, and is followed by India as the world's third largest national economy.

The substantial weight of China in the global economy and its lesser but important weight in global equity indices should give reason to pause. Investments in every country can be adversely affected by changes in government policy. Chinese business seems subject to state direction to a much greater degree than in other major economies. We would urge caution before allocating to Chinese listed equities in line with the likely evolution of China's importance in the global economy.

Some industry experts argue that earnings growth of Chinese equities has been undermined by dilution, as more shares are issued to help fund further growth. The driver of share price performance is earnings per share, and this has been disappointing given the strong earnings growth of Chinese companies. In part this may reflect inefficient allocation of capital by Chinese businesses. If investors want to benefit from China's higher economic growth rate, targeting products sought by Chinese consumers, and sold by foreign companies, may be better than investing in Chinese growth.

The world is changing rapidly, and investors need to be aware and comfortable with how far and why they are over- and under-representing different parts of the global economy, and different regions and industries within global stock markets. In this chapter, we have argued that the diversification benefits of a fully global equity tracker fund often make it a sensible way to invest in equities and any tilt that reduces diversification should be carefully justified.

Investors who wish to let ESG considerations influence their investments should expect that it will lead to different performance, but they should not assume that this will be better performance. The academic division of portfolio risk into undiversifiable, systematic market risk and diversifiable, idiosyncratic risk, though simple, can provide a helpful framework for understanding these differences in performance and risk that ESG-driven adjustments introduce to an investor's strategy. This is seen most clearly when the performance and investment holdings of an investor's equity exposure are compared with those of the global equity index.

9

Risk assets: global credit

In bad times, corporate bonds always show their intrinsic and unhelpful link to stock- market volatility

As we've seen, many lessons have been learned by investors from the credit market disruptions of early 2020 and the global financial crisis of 2007–9. One of the most important lessons for bond investments is that credit portfolios do not need to be complicated, though they often are. This chapter provides an overview of credit and credit ratings and why investors may not receive the premium return suggested by superior yields offered on credit, such as corporate bonds. It introduces the concept of securitisation, which is the process of turning pools of loans (such as mortgages) into marketable securities, and gives a brief introduction to the world of credit derivatives, which are used extensively in the management of credit portfolios.

Advisers sometimes list an investor's exposure to corporate bonds as part of their allocation to cautious or even safe-harbour assets. We think that this is misleading. Well-diversified credit is less volatile and so less risky than equities, but it is safest to assume that any allocation to credit is part of an investor's allocation to risk assets.

This is because corporate bonds and other forms of credit risk should always be expected to underperform government debt in bad times. The intuition is straightforward. When investors buy a corporate bond, they are agreeing to receive a premium yield (the credit spread) over safe government bonds in return for providing insurance for the value of the company up to the value of the bonds that it has issued. If the company fails, they may lose the value of the bond. When the company (as is usual) survives, the investor collects the government bond yield plus a modest premium. In financial market jargon, investors in corporate bonds are writing or selling an option (a put option) on the company.[1]

This leads to some important messages for investors. First, any corporate bond fund should be expected to underperform when stock market volatility increases. Equally, if stock market volatility is unusually low, then the spread over safe government bonds for investing in corporate bonds is also likely to be unusually low. As was seen in early 2020 and in 2007–9, investors should not rely on corporate bonds to have stable capital values at times of stock market turmoil. Although credit is typically less volatile than equities, and the income from diversified corporate bond funds is more resilient than fluctuations in the prices of corporate bonds might suggest, it is still a risk asset.

Years before advances in understanding the pricing of financial options, John Maynard Keynes reviewed a study of long-term returns from equities and bonds in the United States between 1866 and 1922. That study showed a substantial outperformance by equities over bonds in periods of both deflation and inflation.

Keynes found this counter-intuitive, his expectation being that a period of deflation would be better for bonds than equities. The pattern that Keynes expected, but did not find in that very early study, was found by Dimson and colleagues in their 2021 *Global Investment Returns Yearbook*. They found that when inflation was lowest both bond and equity returns were higher than average. So, low inflation was accompanied by good investment returns. But they also found that bond returns exceeded equity returns by almost 6% per year during those low inflation or deflationary years (the bottom 5% of years by rate of inflation). By contrast, at higher rates of inflation, equities on average significantly outperformed bonds.

Keynes suggested several reasons for expecting an inferior performance by bonds.

■ One is the asymmetrical threat of changes in the price level. Bonds can be eroded by inflation without limit, but the scope for negative inflation (which would help bond holders, so long as bond issuers can repay these higher real values) is more constrained.

■ Although a bond may default, no bond ever pays more than its coupon (its predetermined schedule of interest payments).

■ Company management tends to side with equity investors rather than with bond holders and, "in particular, management can normally be relied on to repay bonds at dates most advantageous to the shareholders and most disadvantageous to the bondholders".

■ Reinvested profits, or retained earnings provide an element of compound growth beyond the dividend yield, and this eventually accrues to shareholders in higher prices (while also making existing bond holders more secure in their entitlement to a fixed income).

This underlies the message of many advisers and a number of academics that the natural habitat for genuinely long-term investors is the equity market. Nevertheless, as we've seen, almost all investors do, and should, seek diversification away from equity risk. When considering types of credit as part of a portfolio, it's important to consider two key elements: the trade-off between credit quality and performance, and illiquidity.

Credit quality and the role of credit-rating agencies

Credit-rating agencies originated early in the 20th century to assess the creditworthiness and publish ratings of securities. In practice, there are two related risks that matter most to investors. The first is default by a borrower. The second is an unsettling deterioration in the assessed creditworthiness of a borrower who nevertheless continues to meet contractual obligations.

Investment managers routinely use the ratings of the leading agencies to measure the credit quality of their portfolios and as thresholds to specify the minimum credit quality eligible for inclusion in particular portfolios. This has given them a pivotal role; in the words of the late Peter Bernstein:

> *The rating agencies contribute ... to market liquidity because they spare investors the trouble of carrying out their own credit research.*

The rating agencies provide invaluable statistics detailing the track record of companies in meeting their debt obligations. This reveals that the incidence of bond defaults is cyclical, and concentrated in economic recessions. When companies do default, investors do not typically lose all their investment. It follows that a long time is needed to estimate whether spreads offered on corporate bonds reasonably reward investors for default risk. Of companies whose debt has been rated by credit rating companies, the overwhelming majority of defaults are by companies that were rated as high risk before they default.

The pattern reported for recent decades by credit rating agencies is also reflected in the pattern over much longer time periods. A 2011 article by four financial economists found that default experience is highly clustered and that, on average in the United States, 1.5% of corporate bonds defaulted each year between 1866 and 2008.[2]

Default is triggered by specific breaches of contracts, such as a late coupon payment. In practice investors recovered on average around 40–50% of the amounts due when a default is declared. This suggests an annual loss rate to investors in all types of corporate bonds of around 0.75% per year. Data from credit rating agency Moody's for the period between 1983 and 2020 are consistent with this, reporting an average credit loss rate of 1.0% for all Moody's rated corporate debt. Over the long term, the authors of the 1866–2008 study found that "credit spreads are roughly twice as large as default losses, resulting in an average credit risk premium of about 80 **basis points**".

A separate issue is that investors in corporate bonds often receive a smaller premium yield over Treasury bonds than the average yield spread on which they will have been purchased. Some performance gap should be expected from the impact of occasional defaults. But the reported impact of defaults has been too small to account for the performance gap shown by careful analysis of the data. The explanation owes much to the credit-quality guidelines of investment portfolios or funds. For example, the managers of investment grade bond portfolios can be obliged to sell when bonds are excluded from the benchmark index. This happens when they are downgraded to a high-yield or speculative rating, and normally when the bonds have less than one year to maturity.

Several authors have highlighted the asymmetry between a bond's underperformance before it is downgraded from investment grade, and conversely, a bond's (possibly the same bond) outperformance before it gets promoted to investment grade from high yield.[3] An investor with a credit-quality guideline which requires the sale of any **speculative grade** bond will lose out by suffering the underperformance before the downgrade and by missing the outperformance of soon-to-be-upgraded bonds.

The investor will also suffer from much larger transaction costs when downgraded bonds are sold. A low-fee index-tracking fund that is mirroring an investment grade bond index will suffer these performance penalties. An actively managed bond fund that tries to exploit this phenomenon confronts a steep performance penalty from high fees. The risk of default, which increases with the maturity of a bond, emphasises the need for any buy-and-hold approach to investing in corporate bonds to be well diversified. The long-run academic research quoted above found that increases in **credit spreads** (and so underperformance of corporate bond portfolios) were not principally explained by an increased likelihood of default.

These results suggested that an increase in spreads is more likely to reflect adverse changes in market liquidity, which a long-term investor should be able to withstand. This is consistent with the severe widening of credit spreads in 2008, and during the early stages of the pandemic in March 2020 and the subsequent recoveries. On both occasions (but not necessarily in future), recovery was supported by the substantial injections of liquidity provided by central banks, which both helped the functioning of securities markets and reduced the likelihood of default risk.

Portfolio diversification and credit risk

The words that rating agencies use to describe **sub-investment grade** debt, such as "speculative", "highly speculative" or "poor quality", fairly describe the risk of individual issues when treated in isolation. The strong language that rating agencies use to describe the risk of individual **high-yield bonds** should remind investors that the only sensible way to invest in such credit risk is through a well-diversified portfolio.

Portfolios of credit issues diversify well in good times. Defaults, fears of defaults as well as flights to liquidity all simultaneously adversely affect the broad range of corporate bonds. So a reliable guide to their risk of loss can only be given by long runs of market experience that illustrate the disappointing performance in severe recessions.

In bad times, increases in spreads and credit losses are typically grouped together, and in addition, recovery rates from bankruptcies may be unusually low. Andrew Ang has concluded that "corporate bonds are (scaled-down) versions of equity risk" and that "corporate bonds have large exposures to illiquidity risk". This reminds us that despite the impression given in good times, when returns from portfolios of corporate bonds (and from many other types of investment) are reassuringly benign, corporate credit always is a risk asset.

Local currency emerging-market debt

Emerging market bond issues have grown considerably since the turn of the century, reaching a total outstanding of $29.6 trillion at the end of 2019, according to the investment managers Ashmore, an amount that represented around one quarter of global bond markets. The generic grouping may suit fund managers, but it does not represent a coherent group for investors. These markets are varied both in terms of their levels of financial sophistication, size and creditworthiness. The total includes much local currency debt that did not meet eligibility criteria (including market liquidity) for inclusion in commonly used market indices of emerging market debt.

Despite this, the enormous scale of emerging bonds that have been issued gives an indication of how the shift in the structure of the global economy, and the rise of China, is changing global finance. In years ahead it may be usual for global investors to have significant allocations to China in global bond portfolios. At the end of June 2022, China represented almost 9% of the Bloomberg Barclays global aggregate bond index, and the United States represented just over 40% and the euro zone 19%. In any event, investors should reflect on the single country risk represented by China.[4]

In the past 25 years a growing number of emerging-market governments have issued debt in their own local currency, targeted at international investors. These steps are responding to a market opportunity that suits both investors and borrowers.

A well-diversified portfolio approach to investing in local currency emerging-market debt can be attractive to a range of investors because:

- yields may be more attractive than comparable dollar debt (though this varies between countries)
- it enables investors to take advantage of any view on the relative performance of the US dollar and emerging market currencies

- it may give a source of efficient investment diversification for any investor.

Such investments may be particularly attractive to investors from emerging economies who have their investment accounts measured and reported in US dollars, and yet their base currency is to a degree ambiguous. Currency risk for these investors is less obvious than it is, for example, for a US resident. For some of these international investors, a portfolio of well-diversified emerging-market debt may offer an attractive way of mitigating some of their exposure to the US dollar.

Securitisation, modern ways to invest in bond markets, and credit crises

In recent decades, innovations in securities markets have transformed investment markets and bank balance sheets. At the heart of this is the process known as securitisation, which occurs when a bank loan is transformed into a marketable security.

For a number of years, securitisation was welcomed as a way for banks to better manage their credit exposures by separating their lending decisions from their need to manage the risks of their balance sheets. This was possible through standardised arrangements that enabled the banks to offload their risk exposures to other banks, hedge funds or other investment funds. Securitisation has widened the range of assets that investors may find within a bond or total-return bond fund.

Mortgage-backed securities

Securitisation was a powerful influence in financial markets much earlier than is widely recognised. In real estate, the invention of the elevator in the late 19th century and the building of skyscrapers led to the emergence of "skyscraper bonds" in the early 20th century. These were commercial mortgage-backed securities to fund, or rather fuel, a boom and then overdevelopment of skyscrapers in New York and Chicago in the 1920s. More tall buildings (of over 70 metres) were built in New York during the ten years after 1921 than in any other decade before or since.[5]

Although taller buildings offered the hope of higher total rent income, many of these buildings were speculative builds which were then unable to find tenants to justify the inflated rents which had secured their financing and construction. Heavy losses for investors in real estate bonds followed. The sector rapidly became toxic, and real estate bonds, which represented almost one quarter of US corporate debt issue in 1925, collapsed to almost zero by 1934.

A major advance was the introduction in 1970 of a mortgage-backed security by the Government National Mortgage Association (Ginnie Mae), whose cash payments to investors represented a direct pass-through of the cash flows of the underlying household mortgages. The principal investment feature of pass-through bonds is that they expose the investor to **prepayment risk**, because household mortgage holders in the United States can generally prepay fixed-rate mortgages without penalty. Individuals prepay for different reasons, but the principal driver is the opportunity to refinance at a lower interest rate and cut monthly mortgage payments, after allowing for fees. Another feature of the US residential mortgage market is that interest and principal payment obligations of mortgage-backed securities issued by the three federally sponsored mortgage agencies are guaranteed by those agencies.

This differentiates mortgages that conform to the loan quality guidelines of the federal mortgage institutions from those that do not. Non-conforming mortgages are known as subprime mortgages. Mortgage-backed securities based on pools of conforming US mortgages did not have the dramatic spike in yields experienced by other credit securities during the credit crunch of 2008–10. In contrast, securities that were based on pools of commercial mortgage-backed securities and non-conforming home equity loans inflicted heavy damage on both bank and investor portfolios.

By the mid-1980s, the pass-through mortgage market led to the development of the collateralised mortgage obligation (CMO). The CMO arranges for the payments from a pool of mortgages to be split into a series of **tranches**, exposed to different elements of mortgage prepayment risk. These developments in the US mortgage market transformed the portfolios of investors in US dollar-denominated bonds. In the years before 2008, the repackaging of conforming mortgages provided the model for related, but increasingly convoluted and often ill-fated, innovations in other areas. The critical difference was that the credit-quality guidelines that have always applied to mortgage-backed securities were absent in these new areas.

Total-return bond funds

Most investors would think it common sense that the manager of a bond fund should try to avoid losing money. They would find it uncontroversial that the performance of bond fund managers should be judged on the investment return that they earn, a positive return being better than a negative return, which managers should attempt to avoid. A total-return bond fund (also known as an absolute-return fund) aims to produce an attractive absolute return in all market conditions.

The obvious alternative is a conventional bond fund, where the manager is likely to be assessed for their performance relative to a particular bond market index. The manager is then reckoned (by their employers at least) to have performed well if their fund's investment performance is better than the chosen index benchmark. If the market does very well, then the manager presumably needs to perform even better to be assessed as skilled. However, if yields rise (as in 2022), then bond indices will decline in value, and the manager by this metric does well if their fund declines less than the market index. More than one money manager attempting to explain how well they have performed in difficult markets will have been asked by sceptical investors, "So where has the money gone?"

The vulnerability of total-return bond funds is that their successful management depends on skill at timing changes in the market environment. To avoid a negative return when interest rates rise, they need to be able successfully to time moves into cash, which for over a decade after the global financial crisis offered negligible returns.

The discussion in Chapter 4 about manager skill introduces a note of caution that should temper expectations of substantial success. It is likely that the marketing track record of a total-return fund may have been flattered by the favourable environment created by years of declining interest rates and rising bond prices. Correspondingly, a time of rising interest rates provides a new buffer of interest income that should make it much easier for managers of total-return funds to register positive performance.

Models behaving badly[6]

Quantitative investment is a term used to describe financial processes or strategies that are principally based on mathematical techniques. The term is often abbreviated to "quant", which is also used as an adjective or as a noun to describe investment professionals who routinely use mathematics in their work.

The use of mathematical models in finance allows decisions to be made in an objective way, without being contaminated by an investor's personal biases (see Chapter 2). So a rules-based decision-making process can have definite advantages – although psychological quirks may, to some extent, have been embedded in the model's own quantitative rules in the first place.

Quant was blamed by some for much of the 2007–9 global financial crisis. One argument essentially says that quants were to blame because their bosses did not understand the models they devised. This has some substance, as the skills acquired or possessed by senior managers rarely involve mathematics, though this varies across different cultures.

An extension of this argument is provided by an often-quoted

2009 article by the journalist Felix Salmon, which went as far as to blame the entire collapse of the global economy on a single formula: the formula underpinning collateralised debt obligations (CDOs).[7] In a CDO, payments from pools of loans (one example being sub-prime mortgages) were divided into different tranches, reflecting the order in which payments were received from debtors into the pool. These tranches were given different credit ratings by the rating agencies, with the first tranche of receipts naturally being rated higher than the next tranche and so on.

These tranches were sold to investors (including managers of credit funds) who will have taken those credit ratings to be a guide to probability of losses. In the event, the modelling that underlay the ratings on such **structured products** turned out to be woefully unreliable. Felix Salmon's article challenged investors to ask when quant might be expected to work and when it might be expected not to work.

Quant: when it works, it works – until it doesn't

There is a common practice in valuing equities that is based on two variables:

- the ratio of dividends to corporate earnings
- the discount rate, typically a premium or margin (to allow for credit risk) over the government bond yield.

Although there are different types of stocks, a fairly homogenous group such as the S&P500 can be treated in the same way. Experts in the field will point to subtleties that emerge within this example, but the key idea here is homogeneity; the more similar different assets are, the more they can be valued by the same formula.

In contrast to equities, bonds are much more heterogeneous (a generalisation that often surprises non-professionals). This is reflected in the nature of quant bond models. These usually require many more resources to build and are more complicated than equity models. In some cases, a separate yield curve is used for each company's corporate bonds, whereas in an equity model there may be one or possibly two such curves. Different models are also needed for different categories of bonds (and for different sub-groups within each category). These categories include corporate and government bonds.

Recent years have seen a new aspect of quant investing. This reflects the exploitation by quant hedge funds of big data and high-frequency trading. They seek to exploit profitable opportunities that computer programmes find. Often these strategies exploit trends or differences in yields. Successful high-frequency trading works, when it works, because not enough time elapses to identify the nature of the process. Superior speed allows the investor to identify the mis-pricings that would normally take time to disappear.

The sole concern of the high-frequency trader is whether something works, not why it works. The modellers are typically mathematicians or physicists, not financial economists. The latter would be interested in analysing attribution of performance to consider whether good performance might persist. The mathematicians would consider this all too slow and beside the point.

Quant managers claim that that their key advantage lies first in identifying apparent mis-pricings, and second (and most importantly) the application of a strategy to a large, and so better diversified, range of investments. It is often argued that this reduces the number of investment views that need to be profitable and also avoids clumsy and obvious trading. This reduces transaction costs and allows faster response by quant hedge funds to market signals that are more difficult to identify by other investors. This then allows mis-pricings to persist, and for the strategy to remain profitable, for longer periods of time. Many quant strategies are, at best, statistical artefacts. If a strategy works, it works, at least until it doesn't.

It is conceivable that these hedge funds fulfil a useful service in providing liquidity to markets. However, the evidence suggests that, at times of emerging stress in markets, these funds dramatically cut back their supply of liquidity. There are also signs that these secretive hedge funds have algorithms that are quite similar. This can cause them to amplify instability, for example if one hedge fund makes a trading mistake. Individual investors will not usually come across such modern quant funds, though they may appear within some sophisticated multi-asset funds (see Chapter 10).

History cautions us that quant managers do not walk on water. In Chapter 1, the importance of financial literacy was emphasised. Confronted with an apparent imbalance of knowledge, investors should not let their eyes glaze over when signing up to an attractive-sounding strategy. If the investment story is not capable of simple and plausible explanation, pass it by. As we have already repeated, the needs of individual investors can also be met by low-fee, simple strategies that are tailored to their own circumstances.

In conclusion, individual investors should understand the different characteristics of government and corporate bonds. High-quality government bonds are a safe harbour that will perform as promised over their lifetimes. They deliver short-term negative returns when interest rates rise, but this locks in the promise of higher returns later on.

Corporate bonds are different. They embrace the risk of failure for which a premium return is offered. Since they are risk assets, they should be expected to underperform in more volatile times. But even then, history shows that a widespread deterioration in corporate bonds is likely to be explained more by a temporary and reversible flight to liquidity and risk aversion rather than the permanent losses that flow from increased bankruptcies. Longer-term investors with a buffer of liquidity can be well placed to weather such storms.

10

Multi-asset funds and alternative investments

Multi-asset funds are often complex, and can be less flexible and more expensive than their keep-it-simple index fund competitors. But they can outweigh these disadvantages by giving access to risks and rewards that are often missed

Multi-asset funds can be one-stop shops to meet all an investor's needs. The cheapest multi-asset or multi-strategy funds are low-cost, index-matching balanced funds. These only invest in stocks, bonds, and cash, and form the heart of easy-to-trade savings and investment plans. Multi-asset funds can also provide access to a variety of alternative investments that are not usually available to individual investors but can deliver an attractive and diversifying return with lower volatility.

Actively managed multi-asset funds are risk products, which typically involve additional risk-taking, and so are vulnerable to disappointment when there is a sudden increase in risk aversion in markets. This is when the portfolio diversification suggested by good times can quickly evaporate. One risk is the vulnerability of some frequently priced, liquid alternative investments to occasional extreme negative results. Another is that the illiquidity of many (but not all) alternatives flatters the apparent risk and volatility through infrequent pricing and reliance on appraisal estimates of value. These are markets that the larger managers can better navigate and to which the more sophisticated institutional investors with their larger cheque books have preferential access.

The defining feature of these *private* investments is that they are not traded on organised markets, and so are not suited for a short-term investment. However, even with illiquid private markets, there is continuous pressure to enable investors to adjust their holdings and for secondary markets to develop.

Alternative investments form a broader category. As well as private investments, alternative investments include some easy-to-trade investments, such as gold, other commodities, as well as real estate investment trusts or REITs (see Chapters 7 and 11) and holdings in liquid hedge funds (see below). They can also include exposure to listed companies whose business is investing in infrastructure, private equity and venture capital.

The mismatch between the liquidity offered by continuous pricing of these listed private equity funds and the illiquidity of the underlying investments is brought into balance in the same way as for REITs. The stock market price always suggests a variable discount (or occasionally a premium) between the appraised value of underlying investments and the market's continuous assessment of its value.

These liquid alternative strategies, often known as "liquid alts", may be packaged as alternative mutual funds; alternative "40 Act funds" in the United States, or UCITS hedge funds in Europe. These give investors much more ready access to liquidity than less liquid hedge-fund, private-debt or private-equity strategies. Their price transparency also facilitates easy comparison with the volatility and performance achieved by strategies of index-matching equities and bonds offered by managers of passive funds.

At their best, actively managed multi-asset funds have industry-leading risk management, using leverage and short selling to optimise their chances of outperforming while managing the scope for underperformance. The wide range of strategies adopted by multi-asset funds means that a title may say little about a particular fund's actual investment approach, expected return, risk, level of transparency or expense. The full burden of fees in these sophisticated multi-asset funds is often difficult to gauge but they always chip away at their benefits. The most sophisticated multi-asset funds are also described as multi-strategy hedge funds.

More typically, multi-asset funds include fewer liquid investments, and the diversification benefits of these more complicated strategies are often less than is claimed, and may be missing when they are most wanted. This unreliable diversification is often driven by illiquidity and infrequent valuations. In normal times, this smoothes reported valuations. But as suggested in Chapter 7, this argument for diversification is false and does not help provide security of wealth or income.

In recent years, advisers have recommended larger holdings of illiquid investments. A wide range of alternative investments can be held in multi-asset funds that are difficult or expensive to sell. These can include direct loans and other private debt, infrastructure and renewable energy investments, exposure to leasing contracts, and even income from music and other royalties. Some of these exposures may be represented by specialist hedge funds. They do give exposure to a broader range of risk assets, but in bad times their contribution to diversification often disappoints.

Different fundamental investment issues arise when a low volatility strategy is underpinned by a technical feature described as *implicit option writing*. This has features similar to an insurance company and involve what is also known as short volatility trades. Most of the time, a steady flow of option premia will give a reassuring positive performance. But in bad times, this will be overwhelmed by exceptional losses. These losses are much less surprising than they seem to be. It is no surprise to the authors that the performance of the index-matching, low-cost multi-asset funds provides a demanding benchmark for active funds with a comparable risk profile.

Private debt

A consequence of the 2008 financial crisis has been a change in the shape of investors' portfolios. The crisis was primarily a banking crisis and regulators responded by tightening regulations that govern banks. The new regulations discouraged risky lending and this led to a shift in the patterns of funding risky companies.

Since 2008, the borrowing needs of many smaller and medium-sized businesses, which had previously been met by bank loans, have been met by direct loans from investors. Companies owned by private equity funds have been prominent in tapping this growing source of funding by launching private debt funds. Individual investors will commonly get exposure to these funds when they have a holding in a multi-asset fund. According to Preqin, a private markets consultancy, private debt funds that had a value of $234 billion by 2008 saw this increase to over $1.2 trillion by March 2022.

Investments in private debt funds often supplement holdings of corporate bond funds. Private loans held by private debt funds range from the secure to the speculative and the risk of a debt fund will reflect the choice of loans included in the fund. They typically pay interest at a margin over a variable benchmark rate. Corporate bonds, by contrast, typically pay a fixed yield. This may make private loans attractive to investors who expect interest rates to rise.

Typical types of direct loan include the following.

1. Revolving secured credit facilities of between five and seven years' maturity to established companies.
2. Private debt used to fund infrastructure development, including renewable energy (including water, sewerage, wind and solar). Infrastructure loans can be long term (over 20 years).
3. Leveraged loans, which are loans extended to companies that already have a high level of debt.
4. Direct lending for real estate acquisitions.
5. Distressed debt lent to companies recovering from a restructuring. These typically have credit spreads of around 10% per annum or more over Treasury bills.

After a decade of rapid growth, by 2021 private debt represented around 10% of the total of corporate bonds outstanding. Private loans are less transparent, less liquid and are normally held to maturity rather than traded. Investors should require a premium yield to compensate for these differences.

Private debt funds are sometimes sold on the prospect for earning secure premium returns from under-researched corners of the market. Most private investors will gain exposure to private debt through modest holdings in very large funds. Private debt funds routinely manage more than one billion dollars, often considerably more. With such large fund sizes, the opportunities to earn excess returns are increasingly competed away.

For more than a decade after 2008, the background of declining yields and ample liquidity provided by central banks created a benign background for debtors and will have reduced corporate bankruptcies. A widespread expectation emerged that private debt offered a surprisingly attractive risk premium. In the years after 2008 investors seem *on average* to have been rewarded with such a premium, whether compared to investment grade bonds or high yield bonds. The future may be less generous.

Data from Preqin and Pitchbook, another private markets consultancy, point to a wide dispersion in returns between debt funds (though like-for-like comparisons are difficult). This suggests that good past average results hide the risk in manager selection. As with all unlisted markets, investors need to be confident that their managers have an edge in selecting loans that will more than offset the fees they charge and the inconvenience of illiquidity and lack of transparency.[1]

The attraction of private debt for investors is the prospect of earning a steady income. This should provide a stabilising anchor to hold alongside more volatile parts of an investment strategy. With modest interest rates, secure income will always be expensive and if it appears attractively priced, the presumption needs to be that it is to compensate for other disadvantages. Illiquidity is one such disadvantage, and with it the inability to easily and at low cost rebalance a portfolio.

Insurance-linked securities

Multi-asset funds continuously search for sources of diversifying income flows, and among the most widely available are insurance linked securities. Catastrophe ("cat") bonds are the common type of insurance product that might appear in a multi-asset fund.

Cat bond investors are compensated with high yields for buying potential risks on losses from catastrophic events from insurance companies. The most common insured risks are hurricane or earthquake losses. Their defining feature is the payment of attractive levels of insurance premium most of the time, with the expectation of occasional large losses. Investors in cat bonds suffered severe losses after a Japanese earthquake in March 2011 and in September 2017 following hurricanes in the United States.

Other insurance risks that can be found in multi-asset funds include life settlements, which are life insurance policies, mostly sourced from the US market, that are cashed in by elderly policyholders in exchange for a one-off payment from the investor.

This payment is normally significantly higher than the surrender value on offer from the policyholder's insurance company. Life settlement funds hold these policies and continue to make regular premium payments, in anticipation of a payout when the insured person dies. Some find these investment products distasteful and there have been examples of elderly policyholders receiving poor advice. However, in principle, they can provide a valuable service to the policyholder and a valuable opportunity for investors. In 2021, the life settlement market had a value of around $30 billion, with annual transactions of around $5 billion. This makes it a niche market, which is likely to be found in relatively few multi-asset funds.

Royalties

Royalties provide an example of other niche markets that are represented in some but not most multi-asset funds. Audio streaming provides a high-profile example. The advent of music streaming services has secured royalty payments for successful musicians for years to come. Investors have responded by offering large sums for the copyright of the hits of popular musicians. Funds of music royalties provide diversified music royalties with stable earnings, which seem largely recession-proof.

There will always be worries, though, about the robustness of contracts in coping with subsequent market changes that may affect the flow of royalty income. The music catalogue of an individual musician is likely to be a wasting asset that will be played less and so earn fewer royalties as time passes. Although the amounts offered for the catalogues of a few successful musicians seem large, they represent a modest investment potential for global investors. These niche funds provide attractive investment characteristics and they do appear in some individuals' investment portfolios. Royalties from sports franchises would also be attractive, but they also are not available in size.

Both music royalties and sports royalties can be particularly interesting as they may provide, in addition to a financial royalty, a psychic or emotional dividend to loyal supporters of a sports club or musician. This can have parallels with the non-financial rewards from owning art (see Chapter 12).

Royalties can also be paid for the use of patents, copyrighted works, other franchises or natural resources and they can provide an alternative source of funding capital for companies. Currently, most royalty securities are a claim on a percentage share in future revenues from specific resources sold by mining and oil companies. The opportunities are quite modest and generally illiquid. Their exposure to the business cycle means that they offer inferior diversification compared with royalties from music, sport and other patents.

Hedge funds and alternative risk premia

Hedge funds represent a category of knowledge-based, expensive investment vehicles that are sometimes held in multi-asset funds. They are private entrepreneurial investment companies that operate with few constraints. A characteristic feature is their ability to have **short position**s in investment portfolios and their use of leverage to amplify returns.

Like the total-return bond funds discussed in Chapter 9, hedge funds are intended to generate positive absolute returns, rather than to beat or match a stock or bond market index. Some hedge fund strategies are illiquid, and their managers require long-term commitments from their investors. But hedge fund strategies based on derivatives and currencies can be bought and sold at will.

The patterns of returns from some hedge fund strategies have direct parallels with returns from equity and bond markets. They often emphasise manager skill by reducing the influence of market returns on the portfolio. Other hedge funds offer new opportunities and patterns of return and diversification that are otherwise difficult to access. Examples include the ability to treat market volatility as an investment to be bought and sold and to exploit trends in its pricing. Another is the skill in following trends and momentum in markets. Other investment styles (such as value and quality) have parallels in equity investing (see Chapter 8) and these equity hedge funds form the vast bulk of the assets of the hedge fund industry.

Multi-asset funds often include strategies to exploit pricing discrepancies between different markets or similar investments. These are known as arbitrage strategies. There is no equivalent to the technical skill and market timing involved in these hedge fund strategies in traditional bond and equity portfolios, and the hedge fund industry's casual use of the word "arbitrage" does not mean that these strategies are low risk. Correspondingly, macro and commodity trading advisers (CTAs, also known as managed futures funds) are other strategies that have no parallel in traditional bond and equity strategies.

In these and other areas, hedge funds provide a risk transfer and liquidity service which before 2008 was provided by investment banks. Hedge funds need considerable skill in providing these services. During the short-lived liquidity crisis of early 2020, it was clear that many hedge fund strategies rely on ready access to liquid markets, especially for leverage. This liquidity was briefly interrupted by the emerging covid-19 pandemic and this gave many hedge funds a heart-stopping shock. They were swiftly revived by the massive liquidity support provided by the Federal Reserve and other central banks. Such issues are of little concern to investors with simple strategies built on stocks, bonds and cash. Whether they realised it or not, they did matter for many investors in sophisticated multi-asset strategies.

Investing in hedge funds often includes a large degree of exposure to equity, credit and interest-rate risk, as well as other easy-to-access exposures such as smaller companies and foreign exchange risk. Investors do not need sophisticated products to access these risks. However, hedge fund investing has two principal attractions:

- access to the performance benefits of exceptional investment management skills, which are rare, difficult to find and command a premium price
- access to alternative sources of market returns, to better diversify investment portfolios which are otherwise dominated by equity, credit and interest-rate risk.

Some of the alternative sources of return (also called alternative risk premia) include collecting different insurance premia, at the risk of suffering occasional large losses. These include volatility and event-driven hedge fund strategies. Volatility strategies include collecting premiums for providing insurance against stock market crashes. Other strategies capture **systematic returns** offered by momentum strategies. These sources of risk and return typically are little represented in most investors' portfolios.

Hedge funds and crypto

The rise of digital currencies and blockchain decentralised records of transactions has attracted much attention from some hedge funds and venture capital managers. Like the old adage about the profits to be made from selling shovels to gold prospectors, many alternative managers see value in crypto-related and especially block-related businesses, even if they doubt the long-term value of digital currencies as an investment opportunity.

The principal motivation for hedge funds seems to be opportunities for arbitrage and to offer market-making opportunities. As liquidity improved in some crypto markets, hedge funds were reportedly exploiting profit opportunities that come from much higher spreads and lesser efficiency than traditional markets.

By contrast, a trend-following hedge fund will search for telltale indications of momentum and predictable behaviour by other market participants. They are unlikely to worry whether economists see any basis for value (see Chapter 5). Some hedge funds have been launched to focus on digital assets. As well as focus on pricing discrepancies and predictable crowd behaviour in any reasonably liquid market, they are likely to be attracted by any scope to lock up access to recurring fee income that long commitment periods might give. These behavioural hedge funds will see crypto markets as ideal for exploiting, using their experience from trading other volatile instruments.

The focus of private equity managers in this area is much more substantial. They are particularly attracted by the scope for block-chain technology to disrupt existing procedures for settlement of transactions and record keeping, especially in finance.

Few hedge funds seem to have significant established long-term positions in cryptocurrencies. A value-oriented hedge fund is unlikely to see any value in cryptocurrencies, and so will be unlikely to hold positions in them. By contrast, individual ownership of cryptocurrencies is widespread. It seems likely that, at different times, over 100 million individuals have at some stage owned at least a small amount of cryptocurrency, most commonly bitcoin.

Aggregate ownership is known to be concentrated in a few large owners known as "whales". A 2021 Fidelity survey indicates more than half of their survey of wealthy families in Europe and Asia, and around half of **family offices** in the United States and 30% in Europe and Asia had direct or indirect exposure to digital assets. Investors often feel that they need to learn about these new markets, and the best way to do this is to dip a toe in the water. This does not mean that they currently form a significant part of many large investors' investment allocations.

Private equity and venture capital

Private equity refers to investments in unlisted or private companies that do not have a stock market listing, and so do not have readily available up-to-date prices.

Venture capital refers to that part of private equity which involves new or young ventures or start-ups. In contrast, businesses held by private equity companies may be substantial long-established enterprises that happen not to have a stock market listing.

Most multi-asset funds will not have an allocation to private equity or venture capital. Some do. If so, this will be as an allocation to one or more private equity or venture capital funds. If these are listed closed-end funds, they will have volatile stock market prices, although they may not be easy to sell, except in modest amounts. Alternatively, the holding may be in one or more unlisted funds which is likely to commit the investor to a long holding period, during which the investor may be obliged to make further investments and with liquidation only possible at a large discount.

The appropriate place for private equity in investment strategy is straightforward. Private equity is what it says. It is equity, and so should form part of an investor's allocation to equity. All the comments about diversification by style, by size and by geography for investing in quoted equities (see Chapter 8) apply to private equity too.

However, as private equity is only part of an investor's allocation to equity, there is no requirement to include in a private equity portfolio all the diversification that is readily available from diversified equities. Investors in private equity should be dispassionate in their assessment of the skill of private equity managers. Diversification can then be assessed by reviewing exposure to all equity markets, both listed and private. Then, when assessing performance, the investor ideally needs to be able to separate the impact of manager skill from that of leverage on the manager's track record. In practice, the best that can be hoped is to gain a general indication of the importance of leverage. The smoothing of reported performance in private equity funds, and the drag on that performance of high levels of fees, obscures the impact of both high fees and leverage.[2]

It is likely that an investor with allocations to private equity will also have an allocation to other private asset classes. Each will use up a part of that investor's notional illiquidity budget, that is their comfortable allocation to illiquid investments (see Chapter 7). This should put some constraint on the investor's appetite to hold investments that are difficult to sell, difficult to rebalance and difficult to value.

These magnitudes matter because investors need to have a feel for how an allocation to private equity is changing the risk that is already present in their allocation to listed equity. A diversified allocation to private equity of, say, 10% of an investor's equity allocation, is likely to have a noticeable, but not transforming, effect on the volatility of the overall equity portfolio. However, if the allocation comprises one or more private funds, it will introduce illiquidity and so a degree of rigidity to asset allocation that, most likely, can only be unwound at significant cost.

It is useful to think of private equity in two distinct parts. The first is start-up venture capital. The second is the market for leveraged buy-outs of existing businesses. In recent years, venture capital funds have predominated among the number of private equity fund launches, but the industry has seen larger buy-out funds as institutional investors have committed an unprecedented amount to private equity funds. Some have seen the increased availability of very large buy-out funds as an example of a broader phenomenon that if there is surge in demand for a scarce product the market is able to provide pseudo-substitutes, usually with properties less good than the original.

Holdings in these funds may appear within an individual investor's actively managed multi-asset fund. In early 2022, industry experts reported that the size of "dry powder" (existing commitments available to fund private equity investments) was more than $1.5 trillion, although other experts have questioned whether this amount will fully materialise. In 2022, dry powder represented an enormous supply of funds that risks bidding up prices and so dampening future investment performance.

Multi-asset funds can provide a one-stop shop for an investor's strategy. They give access to risks and rewards to alternative investments such as private equity, venture capital, REITs, infrastructure and commodities, which are missing from the inexpensive low cost, market index strategies of equities, bonds and cash. But it is worth remembering that actively managed multi-asset funds are risk products. Their diversification benefits may lead to disappointment when there is a sudden increase in risk aversion or awareness of actual risk-taking in markets.

11

Home ownership and real estate

Property is at the heart of everyone's finances and well-being

Patient individual investors in real estate investment trusts (REITs) can be in a stronger position than many institutional investors to benefit from investing in real estate

Residential real estate: "There's no place like home"

Everyone needs a home, and the wealth committed to a family home is frequently the biggest single element in household investments. At first glance, many of us allow housing to unbalance our portfolios although, as others have noted, the share of housing in personal wealth is bound to be large, whether or not it is a good investment. This is because home ownership (unlike purely financial investments) serves two roles: it is an investment, but it is also what economists call a "consumption good". If the roof over someone's head is not owned, it must be rented. If it is rented, then the individual has a commitment or obligation to pay rent in the future.

There is an emotional as well as a financial aspect to a home. This can apply whether the property is owned (typically with the help of a mortgage) or rented. The psychological need to make a house a home has parallels with the rewards from owning collections of treasured possessions, such as works of art, which we discuss in Chapter 12. This emotional attachment means that financial calculation may not fully explain why some decide to buy rather than rent a home and why they choose the home they do.

One of the attractions of home ownership is that it provides a hedge against the obligation to pay rent in the future and against unfavourable future house price movements. Although individual house prices are volatile and risky, an investment in housing provides something of a safe harbour and can be less risky for an individual than investment in other risky assets that might be in their savings and investment portfolio.

Families and individuals always need shelter, but the extent of their needs can change with circumstance. Young families will typically need a larger investment in housing than their grandparents. This provides a rational economist's justification for suggesting downsizing in later life. As family size decreases when children leave home, for example, the house becomes proportionately less a safe harbour and more a risky investment. Downsizing can free up financial resources and facilitate a more efficiently balanced portfolio of household wealth.

The years after the global financial crisis of 2008 saw easy money and ultra-low interest rates lift almost all asset prices. The impact on housing generated large windfall gains for home owners. The pattern of home ownership has always varied between countries, influenced by differences in custom, property taxes, and the details of lease agreements. Germany and Switzerland have rates of owner occupation of around 50% and 40% respectively, whereas in the United States and the UK the ratio is noticeably higher at nearer 65%.

The home rental sector has attracted the growing interest of institutional investors so far this century, with both multi-asset hedge funds and traditional asset managers, such as insurance companies, investing in build-to-rent single or multi-family apartment blocks. Sometimes they acquire existing estates (for example, apartment buildings) as going concerns, whose performance they expect to improve. Individual investors might see allocations to such funds within their holdings of multi-strategy funds. This represents the crossover between housing and the broader market for commercial real estate.

Commercial real estate

The commercial real estate market is divided into several main types of property: offices, retail and industrial. Hotels and residential, including apartment buildings and farmland, are also included. The importance of each type of property varies by country. The UK, for example, has been unusual in having had little institutional investment in housing. In recent decades, private equity funds and hedge funds have become important participants in both commercial and residential real estate markets.

Entrepreneurial real estate managers have always liked real estate for the same reason that money managers of any asset class do: they see it as an opportunity to use their skills to make money for themselves and their clients. As the real estate market is such a heterogeneous, lumpy and immobile market, it provides a natural habitat for well-informed, skilled managers to add value – and for other market participants to underperform.

Private equity and real estate hedge funds have brought a more aggressive attitude to leverage in real estate investments. They have also deployed much larger resources that have appeared less price sensitive, and so have driven market prices higher. It is difficult, though, to untangle cause and effect. Low interest rates have encouraged all investors to be willing to pay higher prices, and this is reflected in new and established property managers seeking to deploy additional funds to real estate.

These developments mean that investors now have new investment vehicles to gain exposure to the commercial real estate markets (including real estate debt, as seen in Chapter 10). Real estate returns have always involved, for good or ill, a large element of manager performance, and this will have been amplified by the increased use of leverage employed by hedge funds and private equity and real estate investment trust managers.

The covid shock and real estate investment

Covid lockdowns in 2020 and 2021 shocked commercial real estate markets, with the financial impact varying from the intensely negative to the strongly favourable. Retail shops (excluding food) and hotels in most countries suffered an immediate shutdown. Lockdowns and social distancing led to an amplification of existing trends towards online shopping as well as click-and-collect and home delivery services. This translated into strong demand for food retail as well as supermarket fulfilment centres, data centres, storage and distribution units and industrial properties more generally. During the pandemic, city centres fell silent as work-from-home guidelines took effect.

The lockdowns varied by country, but many businesses were soon unable to pay the rents due on their premises, despite varying degrees of emergency government support. For many office workers outside essential services, working from home became the new normal for almost two years.

In brief, it was a time of extremes for real estate investors. This was not just a hiccup that interrupted usual business: the covid-19 pandemic has significantly accelerated existing trends in real estate. Town centres and shopping malls were already under severe pressure from the long-standing moves toward online shopping. In the late 20th century city centres often showed how they could revive themselves by transforming old industrial premises, close to city centres, into new residential areas as well as technology and arts hubs. A similar process of revival and change is now likely for some older city centre office buildings. This will be encouraged by the difficulty of adjusting older buildings to new environmental standards.

Investments in offices held up well during the early stages of the pandemic, with few interruptions to rent payments. But doubts soon emerged about the demand for office accommodation after the pandemic. Good internet connectivity meant that employers found staff could work effectively from home and they neither needed nor wanted to be in the office five days a week. A wide range of firms discovered they could, at least temporarily, shift some of the burden of renting office space onto employees working from home and a major uncertainty for investors in office real estate emerging from the pandemic was the extent to which this change in work patterns would become a permanent legacy. As the global economy emerged from lockdown, labour markets around the world were unexpectedly tight and it was soon clear that office employees were in a strong position to influence their working conditions.

At present, owners of city-centre offices confront the twin challenges of attracting staff back to the office while financing the cost of ever-tougher building standards to meet the threat of climate change. Although estimates vary, the construction, heating, cooling and lighting of buildings is estimated to contribute almost 40% of global greenhouse gas emissions.[1] There will need to be a major change in building construction and operation if governments are to meet their commitments towards keeping the increase in global temperatures to below 1.5°C above pre-industrial levels.

The values put on existing commercial buildings and the design of new ones is adjusting to this changed environment. The need to adapt to new environmental standards and changing work preferences represent costs to investors, with the risk of fines for non-compliance with new and evolving regulatory standards. These costs are likely to be prohibitive in older city centre offices with many facing the prospect of demolition.[2] Rarely has the old saying that "depreciation is real estate's dirty little secret" been so true. The cautionary note for investors with large exposures to older buildings in city centres, retail malls or town centres is that the cost of renewal falls on them.

What is a commercial property worth and how much return should you expect?

One of the attractions of real estate investing is that it is often easy to produce a plausible simple model to evaluate the finances of a property investment. This is no guarantee of investment success, and spreadsheet jocks can easily miss the importance of non-standard clauses in contracts, but it can help to identify opportunities that rely on unusually strong assumptions.

The financial appraisal of a building needs numbers put on several variables:

- today's rent
- the prospects for rent in years ahead
- today's government bond yield
- tenant creditworthiness and lease terms
- property depreciation or obsolescence.

The reliable rule of thumb is that, like other investments, no real estate investment should be undertaken unless it is expected to perform better than the guaranteed return from high-quality government bonds.

The value of the property is the discounted value of the rent, net of expenses, plus the proceeds from selling the property at some date in the future. In turn, the key variables in forecasting the sale price are the future rate of change in rents, the appropriate rate at which to discount that rental income, and the level of expenses that must be incurred to maintain the building. Detailed projections for local or regional real estate markets can provide inputs for these forecasts. Rents need to be forecast, either implicitly or explicitly, for long periods, so how they relate to inflation provides a useful plausibility check. Not surprisingly, the announcement of tighter environmental standards can have an immediate impact on real estate financing.

This focus on rental income is important to avoid two common mistakes.

First, the value of a property often has little to do with its rebuilding cost. It is the value of future rent that determines its value. Given the value of the property, this can be broken down into the cost of rebuilding, proxied by the insurance value put on the property, and a residual, which is the value of the land underneath the building.

Second, a property is never expensive because the land underneath it is expensive; it is always the other way round. Land is expensive because rents are high; because rents are high, property is expensive.

A third important feature for real estate investing follows from this: the price of land, the residual in property valuation, can be extremely volatile.

A simple illustration is given in Table 11.1.

TABLE 11.1 **The volatility of development land**

	Initial values	Subsequent values
Property value	$10m	$9m
Cost of rebuild	$8m	$8m
Land value	$2m	$1m

Source: Authors' illustration

In this example, if the value of the property declines by 10%, and if rebuilding costs stay the same, the value of the land will halve to $1 million. Conversely, land prices can accelerate rapidly in rising markets. This illustration is important both as an explanation for the speculative nature of development land and as a useful cross-check on valuations. Equally, the importance of the price of land will depend on its scarcity. Where land is abundant and planning restrictions do not impede new construction, rents will tend towards reimbursing with a normal profit the marginal cost of new building, which may or may not keep pace with the general level of inflation.

So long as this situation persists, land will always be inexpensive. With technological progress in building, commercial properties risk becoming a commodity that individuals or corporations who need to use real estate (for homes, offices, industrial or retail space) must decide whether to own, rent or lease on the same basis as other financial decisions. Although rents, and the cost of land, will move with changes in supply and demand, there is no inexorable tendency for them to increase faster than inflation.

Rents can lag behind inflation for a long time. For example, at the height of a boom in City of London property in 1973, rents were reported to have been in the region of £20 per square foot. Allowing for inflation, prime rents in the City of London half a century later, for very much better equipped offices, are less than one third of that level. Property experts will point to various reasons for the underperformance of London City offices, such as the move of the fashion conscious to London's West End and the move of investment banks and the budget conscious to the Docklands financial district.

The investment message, though, is to challenge any assertion that property rents will necessarily keep pace with inflation. There is also little reason to expect them to increase, as is sometimes suggested, in line with the rate of growth of the economy, although it is likely that local population trends can have a major impact over time. It follows that real estate investors rely on rental income, rather than capital appreciation, as the principal source of investment performance. This also explains why the income yield from real estate investing is normally much higher than the income yield from mainstream equity investing.

It is not clear how much premium return over government bonds should be expected by real estate investors. This required premium is reduced by the diversification benefits that real estate brings to a balanced investment strategy. It can also be influenced by the confidence that investors have in picking a skilled real estate manager. Most importantly, as with all private market investments, direct investors in real estate should not assume that they will earn the market return. The prerequisite is to put in place a demonstrably skilful investment process.

The more skill that real estate investment managers (or any private market managers) assume that they have, the easier it will be to justify a large allocation to real estate (or other private markets). In this case, great caution needs to be exercised in assessing the basis for a belief that the manager can access unusual skill. Care is needed in interpreting past performance, in isolating the effects on performance of leverage during a rising market and in differentiating between skill and luck. As was emphasised in Chapter 6, in the presence of uncertainty, the prudent approach is to err on the side of caution.

Private and public markets for commercial real estate

Individuals gain exposure to real estate markets through their homes, and also through home extensions, holiday homes and buy-to-let residential properties. They gain exposure to commercial real estate primarily through investments in real estate investment trusts (REITs).

REITs are stock market listed property companies that need to distribute to shareholders the bulk of their earnings (and in return enjoy limited tax privileges). The attraction of REITs in providing a continuous market for investors was discussed in Chapter 7. This was contrasted with the challenges faced by traditional property funds. Many investors also have exposure to real estate through their holdings of multi-asset funds, which, in turn, may also hold REITs.

Inflation and real estate investing

In recent decades, the income return for REITs has been broadly comparable to that on investment grade bonds. A recurring argument in favour of real estate investing is the provision of a dependable income that can be expected to increase in line with inflation. Bonds, by contrast, are eroded by any unexpected inflation.

Rents from real estate should be expected to respond over time to inflation, but this does not mean that rents will necessarily keep up. This was illustrated with the above example of City of London office rents; a market with excess or obsolete capacity should expect to see rents fall.

Nevertheless, a reasonable assumption is that rents will increase faster the higher is the rate of inflation. This in turn will be reflected in the value put on buildings, which should also respond to inflation. In this way, long-term investments in real estate provide an element of insurance against the biggest danger facing long-term investors in conventional bonds: erosion of wealth by unexpected inflation. As investors have seen, though, inflation linking is far from assured, and it is common for the practical importance of the linkage to be overrated.

REITs differ from old-style property funds (some still found in the UK) in having volatile prices. The income yield from a REIT may be comparable to a corporate bond, but a REIT's volatility is closer to stock market volatility than to the low volatility of a high-quality corporate bond. Consequently, a REIT should not be regarded as a close substitute for an investment grade bond fund.

The volatility of a REIT reflects the need continuously to balance buyers with sellers. This volatility is amplified by varying amounts of leverage that REITs employ. (This is typically around 25–30% with 40% considered a high level). By contrast traditional property funds typically hold a buffer of cash reserves to help meet withdrawal requests. If leverage magnifies a REIT's performance and volatility, cash management normally dampens the investment performance of an old-style property fund, though differences in the types of properties held often makes individual comparisons difficult.

The parallel private and public markets for real estate invite comparisons of where it is cheaper to buy exposure to real estate: by buying REITs or by directly buying properties. In theory, the market price of the REIT should reflect the price of buying the underlying portfolio of properties. In practice, there are always discrepancies. The greater liquidity of REITs might normally cause them to trade at a premium to net asset values, and on average they have done.

International diversification of real estate investment

Real estate investments have traditionally been made in an investor's home country. A 2013 MSCI survey of pension and sovereign wealth funds from 28 countries found that home-country investment accounted for 83% of their real estate exposure. Individual investors will have a strong domestic tilt in real estate investments through their homes and also through holdings in domestic REITs or old-style property funds.

The spread of REIT markets around the world, and the arrival of global real estate hedge funds this century, has facilitated international diversification. We argued in Chapter 8 that hedging international equity investments for currency risk normally has little effect on the volatility of the equity investments: equities are volatile investments whether or not they are **hedged** for currency risk. This also applies to REITs, which have a similar volatility to equities.

However, hedging REIT investments is probably not necessary for a further reason. REITs are commonly leveraged, by securing local currency mortgages on the properties they own. Leverage always increases volatility. However, it helps mitigate volatility that there is normally no mismatch between the currency of the mortgage and the building itself. In practice, globally diversified exposure to REITs is volatile, has a variable income yield and is not normally hedged back to the investor's home currency. Leaving this exposure unhedged will be simplest and is likely to be appropriate. It also gives exposure to the diversifying benefits of global property.

How much should an individual investor allocate to real estate?

An individual investor's allocation to real estate should take account of the existing investment in their home. A decision to make further allocations to real estate should reflect:

- the investor's attitude to risk and the asset's expected performance (relative to safe assets)
- the risk of performance not living up to expectations
- how its range of likely performance outcomes correlates with other investments
- whether the investment is liquid (that is, whether it helps or hinders the investor's flexibility)
- whether such an investment is consistent with any non-financial objectives deemed important by the investor.

Real estate investments illustrate the challenges in trying to have more than an approximate answer to these questions. Quantitative models and investment allocation optimisers are helpful in pulling together the available information, but it is easy to ignore the degree of uncertainty in any calculated allocation. In practice, institutional investors often view income-generating real estate portfolios as an alternative for part of their natural allocation to fixed income. Individual investors need to keep a close watch on diversification of income from real estate, especially if they own rental properties.

Investors in REITs benefit from readily available market prices. This helps calibrate risk much better than if the investor was buying buildings or even an old-style property fund (which relies for prices on surveyors' valuations). Individual investors in REITs always know the market value of their investments and can expect to be able to increase or sell their holdings promptly and for a modest transaction cost.

Institutional investors cannot expect to sell or buy buildings with no delay and they face a large transaction cost each time they buy or sell a building. Individual investors who venture into buy-to-let properties must confront challenges similar to an institutional investor buying and selling, for example, office blocks. They face an uncertain "time on market" when they endeavour to buy or sell and also heavy transaction costs. The effect of these hurdles is to extend the length of time that individuals (and institutions) ought to expect to own individual properties. It is different for a REIT investor for whom these costs of time and money are folded into the price of the REIT.

We've seen that investments in REITs differ from direct investment in buildings by being continuously valued and highly liquid. However, recent research has shown that they gain similar investment exposures as institutional direct investment in real estate if they maintain their investments for a number of years.

Academics have compared the diversification role in a multi-asset strategy of investing in REITS with direct investments in real estate (for a large institution, but there may be lessons for buy-to-let investors). A fair comparison needs to correct for the smoothing effect of surveyors' valuations on direct real estate, and allow for occasional swings in market liquidity and the impact of leverage on REIT performance. Studies that do this are strongly supportive of the diversifying role of real estate in investor strategies which include other alternative assets as well as stocks and bonds.[3]

More recent research has shown that investors who primarily invest in real estate through stock market listed REITs can also benefit from this contribution to diversification from real estate. Using annual performance data for both REITs and direct institutional property portfolios from the United States, the UK, Australia and continental Europe, researchers have shown that, after allowance is made for the leverage of REITS, the performance and volatility of both direct and listed property investments are similar. Both show similar reactions to economic shocks (for good and ill). It also shows that listed and unlisted real estate behave increasingly alike as the holding period increases. Although REITS are stock market investments, they can provide increasingly effective diversification when held with broad stock market investments.

This is not the experience that should be expected with short holding periods, but it is evident as the holding period increases. Investors in REITs have the added advantages of continuous pricing and the flexibility to adjust their investment at any time. They enjoy a privileged position in escaping the constraints imposed on institutional direct investors (and individual buy-to-let investors) of illiquidity, immobility and indivisibility, while benefiting from exposure to the factors that drive real estate returns over time.

12

Art and investments of passion

Investing in things you enjoy owning or supporting gives you more than just monetary rewards

An important historical source of detailed information on the prices of fine art is Gerald Reitlinger's study *The Economics of Taste*, which traced "the rise and fall of picture prices" after 1760.[1] One illustration he gave was of a pair of paintings by Claude Lorrain, a French 17th-century landscape artist, which were sold together in 1808 for £12,600, making them then, he said, among the most expensive paintings ever sold, the price being equivalent to roughly £1,200,000 in 2022 prices. The same paintings were sold together 140 years later for £5,355, equivalent to £207,000 in 2022 prices.

Great paintings bought at a high price can represent an appalling return on money, even if held for a great length of time. This was confirmed by research early this century which indicated that underperformance of the broader market by a masterpiece is not unusual. It found that indicators suggesting high quality for a work of fine art (such as the purchase price of the painting or the number of scholarly citations or the number of exhibitions featuring the work) provide no assurance that the work is going to outperform the rest of the art market in the future. On the contrary, it might perform considerably worse.[2]

Some argue that the difficulty of valuing art, outside auctions, makes the art market prone to bubbles. The central role in pricing by public auction also may make it less likely that a great painting would consistently outperform the broad market.[3]

Many people have collections of paintings, other works of art or items such as stamps, rare books, classic cars or fine wines on which they have expended significant amounts of money. Such collections are sometimes called investments of passion, but they are primarily treasured collections. Some fine art maintains critical appreciation from generation to generation and so keeps a significant monetary as well as aesthetic value, and some contemporary art has appreciated significantly. But this is not the fate of the art that most art lovers buy.

Consistent anecdotes from a range of markets indicate that only a few acquire fine art or collectibles solely to earn a financial return. The prospect of earning an emotional, not financial, dividend from owning a beautiful work or a prized possession is the catalyst for a decision to buy. This is just as well. Researchers have calculated that there were approximately 4,000 artists working in late-19th-century France, who probably produced about 20,000 paintings for sale each year between them. The overwhelming majority of these pictures seem to have disappeared without trace. At that time, perhaps similar numbers will have worked as artists in other countries, including the UK and the United States, and their work also must have largely disappeared. It is sobering to reflect that most art will fall in value to zero when it is no longer enjoyed. It then seems to get discarded.[4]

This does not mean that the purchases were ill advised. It means that they are better seen as consumption goods, which were bought to be enjoyed, rather than investments bought in a realistic expectation of eventually being sold. Our grandchildren's grandchildren will most probably want to buy different treasured possessions.

Headlines from successful auctions are always suggestive of buoyant art markets. In recent decades there have been some eye-catching, seemingly watershed auction results. These include the British artist Damien Hirst's Sotheby's auction in September 2008, on the day that Lehman Brothers failed and proclaimed the arrival of the global financial crisis.

Hirst's auction nevertheless raised $200 million for 223 new works by the artist, and was the most successful single artist auction at the time. Others were the sale in November 2017 for $450 million of Leonardo da Vinci's *Salvator Mundi*, and the sale in March 2021 of the non-fungible-token (**NFT**) *The First 5000 Days* by the artist Mike Winkleman, also known as Beeple, for $69 million.

A number of different art market index providers, each following slightly different methodologies, indicate that the market as a whole has been less buoyant than might be thought since 2008. But contemporary art has been booming, after a sharp setback in 2009–10.

Technology, NFTs and the art market

The making, buying and recording of much art has been transformed this century by digitalisation, and the enormous improvements in transparency made possible by the internet. Technology has enabled new media including Hockney's iPad drawings and the range of digital art. The internet has brought global reach to the humblest local auction house. It helps transparency of auction pricing and record keeping. It facilitates fractional ownership of masterpiece works of art with blockchain records of transactions able to underpin authoritative records of provenance and title.

Auctions of digital art are a regular feature in the contemporary art market. In 2021, digital art is estimated by Artprice.com, an art market consultant, to have accounted for 8% of global auction house turnover. Non-fungible tokens (NFTs) are unique digital certificates that confirm ownership of the only digital record of a digital asset, such as a digital work of art. NFTs grew out of the world of online gaming and the minting (creation) of unique tokens or sought-after collectibles of digital art within an online game. Leading art galleries have used the innovation to develop a new source of revenue by auctioning or selling unique digital copies of works of art from their collections. The owners of leading newspapers have auctioned NFTs of cover pages from notable dates in history.

A characteristic of digital art is that it can be copied and reproduced with no change of quality. However, only the owner of the NFT will own the underlying computer code (hence, it is non-fungible). It does not indicate copyright of whatever images are included in the NFT and instances have been reported of artists being surprised to see their art included in NFTs.

Ownership of an NFT conveys quite limited ownership rights. In the words of one leading auction house, ownership of an NFT allows you to "display the digital work for your own personal and non-commercial use ... you do not receive any intellectual property rights in the digital work". The auction house goes on to advise that "generally, anyone can download and share a digital work with which an NFT is associated".[5]

NFTs are being used in digital registries for both digital art and conventional works of art. Artory, a blockchain-secured digital registry for art and collectibles, has attracted funding from venture capital investors seeking to establish a record of verified history or provenance for both digital and conventional art.

The digital ledger brings improved confidence in ownership, a prerequisite for the development of services in art ownership. In turn, this helps owners of collections of fine art secure loans and it encourages, for example, the development of fractional ownership of works of art, which then can have multiple owners. It could, for example, allow you to buy 0.1% of an Andy Warhol.

Separately, Masterworks.io has raised funds to acquire selected contemporary works of art to offer for fractional ownership. It then offers each painting that it buys for fractional ownership at a stock exchange listing (that is an IPO, or initial public offering). It invites subscriptions from those who have pre-registered on their platform, giving an expected life for the limited company owning the work of art of between three and ten years.

There may be scope to sell a fractional holding on the Masterworks internal secondary market, with transaction costs less than would apply if the painting is sold at public auction. However, the expectation is that investments will be held for the life of the limited company. A major attraction of this is that investors are able to acquire shares in the works of selected well known contemporary artists for much smaller amounts than purchasing the entire painting. A share in a Banksy might be bought for $1,000 rather than over $1,000,000 that the original might cost. The Banksy would be professionally stored, but it would not decorate your wall. The platform charges fees that are comparable to those of private market investment funds.

The rise of online sales

The covid-19 pandemic accelerated the trend towards innovation in online transactions, auctions and exhibitions of art and other investments of passion. In 2021, online sales of fine art reached $13.34 billion, equivalent to about 20% of total sales by galleries, dealers and auction houses.[6] Dealers and auction houses report that the pandemic led to an influx of new buyers, bidding in online auctions at all price levels. It has given a lift to turnover and liquidity in markets for investments of passion. Lockdowns encouraged auction houses and online apps devoted to niche luxury markets to improve their online services, and this has improved the liquidity of their markets.

The recent benign climate for investments of passion

The first two decades of this century were remarkably favourable for investments of passion. In addition to the greater depth of markets provided by the rise of online trading, the persistence of negligible yields on cash savings, a global rise in wealth (and in wealth inequality) have all favoured these markets.

Any purchase involves choices. By purchasing a painting, a collector decides to forgo the interest that could be earned on cash or from holding bonds of roughly the maturity in years that the collector might own the painting. Collectors buy paintings because they prefer the prospect of enjoying the art at least as much as they would benefit from the interest income that they forgo when buying it.

The world's high net worth families hold almost one quarter of their financial wealth as cash or near-cash (see Chapter 6), and so the income of these families will vary by over $100 billion per year for each 1% change in cash deposit rates. When interest rates fell to around zero, as they did for over a decade after 2008, it was much easier to justify spending money on art or a luxury watch, another collectible or almost anything rather than leaving the money in the bank.

A different angle on the same phenomenon is seen by looking at the impact of income and wealth inequality on the demand for luxury goods and fine art. Academic research published in 2011 explored the relationship between art prices and the economy.[7] It found that during the past two centuries equity market returns have had a significant impact on the price level in the art market. Another finding was that an increase in income inequality may lead to higher prices for art, and a strong suggestion of a long-run relation between top incomes and art prices: when high-end incomes increased much faster than average incomes, art prices tended to respond strongly.

This has been seen in the patterns of art market booms and stagnations over the past 150 years. The longest period of cumulative underperformance by art prices was in the decades after they reached a peak level in 1914. That level was not reached again, after inflation, until a strong recovery in the 1960s. The intervening long period of stagnation occurred despite personal income rising almost fourfold. It was, however, a period when income inequality declined sharply, eroding the relative buying power of the wealthiest.

The past 150 years show that a disappointing environment for the art market can persist for decades. After the 1970s, fine art prices easily outpaced inflation, supported by much higher top incomes, and climbed to levels not seen before. Despite this, there have been significant setbacks in the overall art market in the past 50 years and marked changes of fashion within it. Other researchers found a similar pattern for prices of stamps and violins over the past century, although their periods of weakness do not always coincide with those in the art market.

These influences on prices for art and collectibles are reflected in prices for luxury goods. Although millions of people reportedly collect assorted treasured items, the top end of each category of luxury goods, be it fine wine, fine art, luxury watches, rare stamps or classic cars, will be influenced by the incomes, wealth and perceptions of competing investment opportunities of the most affluent. The fluctuating spending power of crypto entrepreneurs and speculators, hedge fund managers, technology titans, Russian oligarchs, Chinese billionaires and national museums has helped to propel prices of luxury goods and art in recent decades.

Price indices for art and collectibles

Recent trends in prices for fine art and collectibles can be seen more clearly thanks to the publication by academics and consultancies of price indices that trace the evolution of their prices often dating back to the start of the 20th century.

Academics have calculated that the average price increase of art, stamps and violins over long periods beat the investment return on cash and government bonds but noticeably underperformed the stock market. Other studies have also placed the price performance of fine art over differing long time periods as being somewhere below that of equities but better than cash.

In practice, the average collector of fine art will not have done so well, because the data take no account of the costs of buying and selling items from their collections. Transaction costs are generally higher in such illiquid markets and can easily be well over 25% of the price of an object offered for sale (see below). As was discussed in Chapter 10, average index returns from illiquid markets are earned by no one and they also hide fluctuations over time and of fashions within it.

Reitlinger's book has proved to be a treasure trove for researchers. Academics have reviewed the evolution of art prices over time (mostly using Reitlinger's data). The conclusion of an authoritative review (now somewhat dated) of these studies is: "All except [one] give the same answer to the question: Is buying art simply to resell at a higher price likely to be profitable? The answer is no."[8]

Psychic returns from art and collectibles

Collectors collect and art lovers buy art because they expect to enjoy their collections. This aesthetic, emotional or psychic reward is a dividend to be valued over and above any monetary return that they might hope to get when (or if) they eventually sell their collection.

A number of economists have attempted to estimate the psychic return from art. Some have used data on the cost of renting art (for example, by corporations) and produced high implied psychic returns, in the order of 10–30% per year. These high figures have been criticised for combining the cost of a valuable consultancy service, which is advising companies or individuals on which art they ought to rent, with the enjoyment that flows from a treasured possession.

A 2013 academic research paper evaluated alternative approaches for measuring psychic returns to cultural assets. After taking into account the substantial transaction costs, apparent long holding periods for works of art and likely proportions of investable wealth invested in art, it found that psychic returns from fine art are probably in the region of less than 1–2% per year of the cost of a painting.

It also found that the long periods for which works of art are generally held mean that the impact of high transaction costs in the art market (for example, commission rates at auction) is less of a burden compared with stock market investing (where holding periods are much shorter) than the headline numbers suggest. Their conclusion was that an annual advantage to investing in equities over buying a painting of between 0.5% and 1% per year seems plausible, if both the painting and the investment in the stock market are held for 20–30 years.[9] But high transaction costs substantially erode potential returns from investing in art and collectibles.

The persistence of value in art

Economics may help explain overall market trends, but it is less clear which criteria explain the financial value of the work of individual artists. The valuation of any painting ought to be an assessment of what someone else would be willing to pay for it, which will be strongly influenced by assessments of its quality. Maintenance of value is likely to be reinforced when critical acclaim for an artist survives from one generation to another.

Several studies have looked for this. One academic study published in 2006 examined the critical recognition of Italian Renaissance artists over the past 450 years.[10] The authors used as their benchmark the prominence given to artists in authoritative art history textbooks at different dates over this period. The measures used were the number of citations and the length of written reviews of each artist.

This analysis started with the assessment published in 1550 by Giorgio Vasari, a notable artist and pioneering art historian. The academics compared Vasari's write-ups with those of six subsequent authorities spread over the centuries since then, ending with *The Grove Dictionary of Art*, which was published as 34 volumes in 1996 and has now been superseded by the regularly updated online edition. The comparison of the different art authorities over time highlights an impressive persistence in the art establishment's apparent rating of the leading figures of the Italian Renaissance. It shows that each of the seven selected authorities from the past 470 years appear to have chosen Giotto, Michelangelo and Raphael as among the top ten Italian Renaissance artists, with five of the seven authorities also including Titian and Leonardo da Vinci.

This pattern of persistent recognition of quality of the top-ranking Italian old master painters demonstrates that some assessments of art quality can be relied on to endure. This helps to underpin the financial value of acclaimed artists from one generation to the next. It seems a reasonably safe bet that a work of art by Raphael will still be prized and highly valued in 200 years' time. An art gallery is unlikely to be embarrassed by owning it, but that does not mean, if it ever came to market, that it would perform well as a financial investment.

In the market for contemporary art there is no history of critical acclaim, and whether a contemporary artist's work is judged by art experts to be strong or weak is largely a matter of subjective opinion. The support of influential opinion formers and patrons has always been important in establishing a halo effect by securing recognition and commercial success for artists. This can take time even for those later acknowledged as masters. The celebrated example, which gives hope to countless yet-to-be-discovered artists, is Vincent van Gogh, who died penniless and apparently sold few paintings during his brief lifetime despite his brother and uncle being art dealers.[11]

Brand is recognised as important in underpinning commercial value in the market for contemporary art. Branding (or, as art market people call it, "validation") can be provided by an artist being supported by a leading art dealer; by work being offered for sale by either Sotheby's or Christie's, still the world's two dominant fine art auction houses; by being exhibited at or bought by a leading modern art gallery; or by having works bought by a celebrated collector. These are the gatekeepers, the most important arbiters of perceived quality in the market.

When a contemporary artist has been validated by several of these, they become a branded artist whose work will henceforth command a higher price. If a collector can anticipate this process by buying pre-branded, yet-to-be-discovered artists, the road to financial success in collecting contemporary art would be secured. In practice, there may be many good contemporary artists, but only a few secure financial success by becoming branded.

Over the ages there have been countless wealthy patrons, collectors and sponsors of art. Among these are some whose collections have subsequently become extremely valuable. There is little indication that a desire to accumulate wealth rather than a love of art motivated their collections, even though history might judge them to have been canny collectors.

An outstanding example of this is the collection of 20th-century art, including some by Pablo Picasso and Jasper Johns, amassed over the lifetimes of Victor and Sally Ganz of New York. The Ganz estate sold 114 paintings at auction in 1997, raising a total of $207 million compared with an original outlay of $764,000. Subsequent auctions of family collections have raised larger amounts. These include the November 2021 auction of part of the art collection of New York real estate magnate Harry Macklowe and his former wife Linda Burg, which included works by Rothko, Pollock, Picasso, Koons and Warhol and raised $676 million.

The Ganz collection has been analysed by academics who found that its performance easily beat investing in the US stock market over the same period.[12] Although data comparisons are difficult, it seems clear that the collection outperformed the wider art market. The analysis found that the financial performance of the Ganz collection was not simply attributable to the extraordinary results from one or two paintings, but showed a degree of persistence from one artist to another and across periods of investing. It also found that these paintings and prints appeared to attract a premium price because they came from the Ganz collection.

Art market auctions: a gold mine for statisticians

Art collectors wish (if only for insurance purposes) to have an estimate of the value of their most treasured works, and the easiest way to estimate value is to take account where possible of the prices achieved by comparable art, at a recent date, at public auction. A development of recent decades has been the compilation by several competing providers of art market indices and online art valuation services.

The role of the auction houses has facilitated the development of these services by providing a degree of transparency to pricing that would not be available if all transactions occurred through dealers' galleries, at art fairs or in auction houses' private sales. However, each of the art indices suffers from weaknesses. Some are common to the measurement of performance in any illiquid market; some are more specific to the art market; and others reflect differences in methodology and coverage. Each of the leading art indices reflects transactions that occur at public auction but not those, by their nature confidential, that occur through dealers' galleries or at art fairs. It is estimated by Arts Economics that public auctions accounted for just under half of the value of the turnover of the fine art market in 2021.

The ready availability of price information (including pre-auction price estimates) makes auctions a gold mine for statisticians and analysts. In some illiquid markets, all transactions are private and indices of market performance need to rely on expert valuations. In the art market, the index providers are able to use auction results. However, as in other markets, the indices exclude the impact on financial performance of commission costs. Typically, the index providers also exclude items that fail to reach their reserve price and so remain unsold (or "bought-in"). They also miss items that are withdrawn from sale immediately before an auction. This may reflect a number of issues, including a concern that demand will be weak. It was not unusual for a third of auction items to fail to reach their reserve price at auction.[13]

Investing in art and collectibles

There has been much talk about investing in art, but apparently little as a purely financial investment. The recent emergence of fractional purchases of individual selected contemporary works of art may represent the start of a new trend. Historically, there have been numerous attempts to launch art funds, with subscribers holding shares in a portfolio of art. One early success dates from 1904, when a French financier and 12 friends formed a fund called, with intentional irony, La Peau de l'Ours (the skin of the bear) after a fable in which hunters sell the skin of a bear which they are then unable to catch. It was a financial success, thanks to shrewd selection of works of art (including from Gaugin, Monet and Matisse) and extraordinary good luck in winding up after ten years, just before the start of the first world war. Art market indices show that this was also a peak level for art market prices that was not reached again, after allowing for inflation, for over 50 years.

Immediately before the 2008 financial crisis, there was a flurry of ambitious plans to launch funds to invest in differing parts of the art market. Since then, art and wealth advisers have launched various private art funds. The focus of art advisers is more commonly advising their wealthiest clients on the management of their art collections, advising on purchases and sales, and the arrangement of credit facilities secured against high-value works of art. Works of art may represent a significant part of the wealth of such investors. Advisers may emphasise the scope to make a profit from their portfolios, but they are often better described as collections, rather than as investment portfolios.

Shared characteristics of fine art and other investments of passion

Investments of passion, or hobby collections, share a number of characteristics.

■ The importance of provenance (that is, authentication and ownership history) of any item cannot be overstated. Even the grandest art collections and galleries run the risk of having major works reassessed by experts. The implications on valuation of having an important work reassessed as "from the school of" rather than by a particular old master painter would be severe; to have a treasured work of art exposed as a forgery would be much worse.

■ Corresponding threats confront a collection of stamps or coins: differences in qualitative assessment can seem arcane to an outsider but can make an important difference to judgments of the quality of a collection. The expertise and the passion of the collector, whether of fine art or collectibles, are directed at minimising such risk. (Philatelists would point out that notorious forgeries of stamps can, in some circumstances, be worth similar amounts to the original.)

■ The asymmetry of information that exists between market insiders and most investors is a feature that is shared with all illiquid markets. Those wishing to build a collection need to appreciate that an informational advantage almost always lies with the market professional.

Transaction costs are normally much higher with art and investments of passion than in more liquid securities markets. At art auctions, transaction costs are dominated by the buyer and seller premia, or commissions. For example, at one of the major auction houses, where the buyer's commission is calculated on a sliding scale, the commission payable for a purchase with a hammer price of $1.5 million could be over 20%, with 26% payable on the first $250,000, even before other taxes.

Commissions payable by the seller (or consignor) of a work are also significant, but since a price-fixing scandal in 2002, they may now be more susceptible to economic pressures. Nevertheless, it is safe to assume that the auction houses may extract 25% of the price of a high-value painting and more for smaller value items. Where indirect taxes are paid on commissions, transaction costs can easily exceed 30%.

Such transaction costs are likely to stymie most approaches to investments of passion that do not involve a patient buy-and-hold strategy. One exception to this is that in some markets (especially for collectibles) auction lots may include a large mixed lot of, for example, cartons of old stamp albums and packets offered as a single lot. Even when one has an accepted method of valuation, the cost of valuing the lot piece by piece is prohibitively high and this is where profit is possible as the return to the expertise needed to value the lot.

Art prices and the "tiny" size of the art market

The financial resources that could in principle be allocated to acquisitions of art are enormous relative to the size of the global art market. Deep pockets in the Middle East are funding new national galleries. More importantly, there is a traditional imbalance between the tiny size of the art market compared with total private financial wealth. Global sales of art and antiques are estimated by Arts Economics and UBS to have been $65 billion in 2021, but investable financial wealth was estimated by the Capgemini 2022 *World Wealth Report* to have been $86 trillion (that is, $86,000 billion), with almost $21 trillion available as cash or deposits.

The insignificant size of the art market, in relation to disposable wealth, means that a move by any substantial investor or group of investors to establish or extend a major art collection is likely to provide considerable support to prices. The easiest way to justify a purely financial investment in sought-after parts of the fine art market would be a belief that prices would increasingly be supported by at least some such investors for decades ahead. As academics have noted, economics is unable to suggest any upper limit for the prices of highly prized art.

Surprisingly, this very indeterminacy enhances the role of experts. In relatively **efficient markets**, such as the stock or bond markets, fundamentals are of considerable importance and known future adjustments to dividends will tend automatically to be reflected in the current price. However, the absence of fundamentals in the art market increases the importance of experts and expert opinion is likely to have a greater role in influencing prices.

A particular application of expert opinion is provided by the company ArtTactic. An important structural feature of the art auction market is the estimated price range supplied by the auction house in advance of a sale. Since 2013, the online ArtTactic Forecaster competition has gathered repeated price predictions from hundreds of self-selected forecasters who choose whichever price range they expect to contain final auction prices for a selection of high-profile lots (in a multiple-choice survey). Predictions are obtained during a period starting a few days before each auction sale.

An interesting finding is that the average predictions of all forecasters, on average, tend to lie very close to the middle of the range of the auctioneer's estimates. This finding appears to be a classic example of *anchoring bias*, as discussed in Chapter 2 and this probably enhances the credibility with which the auction houses are regarded.

Surprising auction price outcomes are the exception rather than the rule, but they are rarely ever predicted by the average of the "crowd" forecast. Greater predictive power requires more measurement, potentially taking into account the skill levels of particular forecasters with respect to specific artists and categories of work. Nevertheless, although the average forecasts may lack significant predictive power over surprises, the variance of opinion among forecasters is arguably more informative.

The modest range of price estimates for most readily traded collectibles (such as Rolex watches) can be contrasted with the wider ranges of expert assessments of value for relatively esoteric pieces. An example is the work by younger artists who are less deeply researched and have shorter track records at auction. Since these predictions involve very short time horizons (such as a few days), they do not convey significant information about the market risk associated with a work of art over the long term.

Long-term risk is challenging to assess as it involves such factors as reputation and changing tastes. However, to some extent, the ranges of expert valuations can be viewed as subjective indications of risk associated with auction sale execution. As collectors are well aware, even when a piece is worthy of inclusion in a sale by a top-tier auction house (which might be taken for granted in the case of prominent works), there is significant uncertainty about its selling price in the room on the day.

Understanding the magnitude of this price risk is an important consideration when lending money against prestigious art as collateral (see below). An expert valuation such as an auctioneer's estimate only tells part of the story. Prediction variance presents one way of assessing this, either in estimated monetary terms, or in terms of ranking against other artists and works. This is closely related to the risk of a lot completely failing to sell at auction (effectively valued by participants at below its reserve price). Taken together, estimates of no-sale probability and prediction range appear to be helpful risk metrics to enhance professional valuations.

Collectibles as collateral

The illiquidity of collectibles represents a serious issue for those who wish to collect and put substantial money into their collections. There have been a number of innovations to address this problem by setting up structures whereby collectors can use their collections as collateral for loans.

Art-secured lending can be seen as an effective way of enabling art collectors to access the equity value in their artworks without having to sell their art, an action that could trigger a tax liability. Art lending makes it possible for collectors to redeploy their capital into new art acquisitions or attractive business opportunities, or to refinance existing loans.

The Art & Finance Report 2021 by Deloitte and ArtTactic estimates the size of the art-secured lending market to have been around $26 billion in 2021 (based on the value of loans outstanding). The valuation of high-value art is a service that is largely provided by private banks and auction houses. It is driven by art being used as collateral for loans.[14] A niche aspect of this service is the valuation of art which is held as an asset by some hedge funds.

Developments in the provision of loans secured against works of art is just one aspect of how the needs of finance are generating change in the art market. As ever, finance is moving in tandem with technology in driving change in the making, recording ownership, valuation and selling of art. Technology is also driving change in understanding the techniques of artists from previous centuries and in confirming attribution. Finance and technology are having an impact in making the markets for fine art and collectibles more liquid, more global, more transparent and more accessible.

Glossary

This glossary does not repeat definitions and explanations of concepts that are provided in the main text.

Active
management

Investment strategies of active investment managers who are appointed in the expectation that they will perform better than the market as a whole, after allowing for the extra fees paid for active management. These strategies always involve avoidable turnover (compared with a passive or market matching strategy) and the avoidable risk of underperforming the market. See also **passive strategies**.

Annualised,
arithmetic
average and
geometric
returns

The arithmetic average performance is the simple average over time of investment returns. This is higher than the compounded or geometric average of returns. The difference is easy to illustrate. Suppose a portfolio performance in one period is -50% and in the next is +100%. The arithmetic average performance is +25% [(−50 + 100) ÷ 2]. The geometric average or compound return, however, is 100 × (0.5 × 2.0) −100 or 0%. Standard risk measures such as the standard deviation should be used in conjunction with the arithmetic average. However, the geometric or compound return describes the evolution of wealth over time.

Annuity

A regular sum of money paid to the holder of an insurance contract, typically by an insurance company. A life annuity is paid for the rest of the policy holder's life.

Asset allocation

Allocation of investments among different markets. Contrast with stock selection, which is the allocation of investments within a particular market.

Base currency

Investors' home currency in which their investment objectives are expressed. Their base currency is normally, but not always, unambiguous. See Chapters 8 and 9.

Basis point (BP)

One hundredth of one per cent: 0.01%.

Beta

A measure of the extent to which a stock might provide diluted exposure (if the measure of beta is less than 1.0) or leveraged exposure (if the measure of beta is greater than 1.0) to equity market risk.

Bonds

See **conventional bond**.

Break-even rate of inflation

This is (approximately) the difference between the redemption yield on conventional government bonds and that on inflation-linked government bonds of the same maturity. If inflation happens to equal the break-even rate, the total return on inflation-linked and conventional government bonds will be approximately identical. See Chapter 4.

Contrarian

An investor, or a strategy, that deliberately seeks to be unfashionable and to go against recent market trends. Typically, this is an adjective that is used to describe value investors; see Chapter 8.

Conventional bond	A fixed-income bond (which has a predetermined schedule of fixed-interest coupons and a fixed redemption value). The word "conventional" is used to distinguish the bond from inflation-linked or floating-rate bonds. Inflation-linked bonds have coupons and/or redemption values that are adjusted in line with inflation. Floating-rate bonds have coupons that are reset in line with a specified short-term reference rate of interest, such as the London Interbank Offered Rate (LIBOR).
Correlation	The degree of linear association between two variables. In other words, it is a standardised measure of the extent to which the prices of two investments move together (but not necessarily by the same amount). The correlation coefficient, R, can vary between −1 and +1. A correlation coefficient of 0 suggests no relationship between the movements in the prices of the two investments. A positive correlation suggests that the prices of the two investments tend to rise or fall at the same time. A negative correlation suggests that the prices of the two investments tend to move in opposite directions at any particular time. Negative correlations are highly desirable in constructing portfolios of risky assets, because they reduce risk. However, negatively correlated attractive investments are rare.
Credit spread	The extra yield offered by a risky bond over that offered by the Treasury for a bond of the same maturity to compensate an investor for the risk that the issue might default. Extra yield may also be paid to compensate for the illiquidity of an issue.

Derivatives	Derived investment contracts, which are designed to replicate certain aspects of risk that can be obtained from direct investment in markets such as equity or fixed income.
Duration	The average life of a bond and also a measure of a bond's sensitivity to movements in interest rates. (Slight differences in calculation are reflected in these definitions.) Duration is the weighted average time to the total of scheduled payments, where the weights are determined by the present value of each payment. Duration is shorter than the maturity of a bond, because it takes account of the earlier dates on which interest coupons are paid. The exception is a zero coupon bond, the duration of which is the same as its maturity. There are two common but similar technical definitions of duration: Macaulay duration, which is most useful in precisely matching a future stream of payments; and modified duration, which provides a measure of the sensitivity of a bond portfolio to small changes in interest rates.
Efficient markets	An efficient market can be thought of, intuitively, as one in which there is no financial advantage to forecasting the future based on past information. An efficient market should have this property most of the time. This need not be true all the time as there are occasions when one can predict what will happen.
ESG	Environmental social and governance in investing. See Chapter 8.

ETF	Exchange traded fund: an investment product that gives exposure to a particular market. The ETF itself is listed on the stock market, and so is highly liquid and generally accessible at modest transaction prices.
Family office	The private office of a wealthy family which is entrusted with the management of the family's financial affairs.
Forward contract	Similar to a futures contract, except that it may not be standardised (though most probably it will be) and does not benefit from the transparent pricing and support of a formal exchange. As a result, forwards may not be marked to market each day. This gives rise to larger issues of counterparty risk than exist with futures contracts, which are transacted on a formal exchange.
Futures contract	A standardised contract entered into, on a futures exchange, to buy or sell a particular investment or basket of investments at a given date in the future. The exchange guarantees payments between members of the exchange (but not their clients). In practice, profit and loss on a futures contract is calculated on a daily basis and reflected in payments of variation margin to and from the exchange's clearing house by both parties to a contract.
Hedged	An indication that market risk, for example from the stock market or a foreign exchange market, has been neutralised using derivatives or other instruments.

Heuristic	A simple procedure that helps find adequate though often imperfect answers to difficult questions. A shortcut.
High-yield bond	A debt issue which is judged by credit-rating agencies to be at best speculative or not well secured. See also **sub-investment grade**, **investment grade** and Chapter 9.
Index investing	Market-matching investment strategies that involve minimal turnover and expense. Turnover typically occurs only to accommodate inflows or outflows of investor funds and to improve the market-matching features of the investment portfolio. Also known as passive investing.
Inflation risk premium	An amount by which the break-even rate of inflation may exceed the expected rate of inflation to allow for the risk that inflation may be higher than expected. See Chapter 4.
Investment grade	The group of credit ratings given by the principal rating agencies to debt securities whose credit rating is assessed as being at least moderate to good quality. This differentiates investment grade debt from issues which are judged to be at best speculative or not well secured. See **sub-investment grade** and Chapter 9.
Large cap	One of the largest companies by stock market capitalisation. In the United States a common definition is that a quoted company is large cap if its market capitalisation exceeds $10 billion. See Chapter 8.
Leverage	An indication of the extent to which an investment, and thus its performance, is geared through the level of debt embedded in it.

Liquidity | An indication of the ease with which investments can be bought or sold at close to their advertised price. In illiquid markets it can be difficult to buy and sell investments.

Long-only strategy | A traditional investment strategy or portfolio consisting only of investments which are owned, not investments which are borrowed or sold short. See also **short position**.

Mean reversion | The belief, fundamental to the outlook of value investors, that prices in financial markets tend to overreact, oscillating between overvaluation and undervaluation. Mean reversion refers to an expectation that expensive markets can be relied upon to become cheaper and inexpensive markets can be relied upon to become priced closer to "fair value".

Meme stock | See Introduction.

Mental accounting | A concept from behavioural finance. The set of cognitive operations used by individuals and households to organise, evaluate and keep track of financial activities.

Money market funds | Funds that invest in cash, cash equivalent securities, and in highly liquid, near-term instruments with high credit rating, such as US Treasuries. Money market funds are intended to offer investors high liquidity with a very low level of risk.

Natural habitat | The natural investment home for a particular investor, such as long-dated Treasury bonds for a pension fund.

NFT | A non-fungible token (NFT) is a unit of data stored on a blockchain, which can be sold and traded. Unlike most cryptocurrencies which are fungible, each token is uniquely identifiable with artworks (photos, videos, audio) and property.

Noise
Meaningless apparent market signals which make it more difficult to interpret market developments. Noise is both a cause and a reflection of uncertainty. One cause of noise is the impact on markets of the transactions of investors who lack insight or who transact for reasons other than in response to market signals (for example, investors who have an impact on markets because, for whatever reason, they need to sell). See Chapter 4.

Option
A contract that gives the purchaser the right, but not the obligation, to buy (call option) or sell (put option) a particular investment at a given price on (if a European option) or before (if a US option) the given expiry date for the contract.

Passive strategies
Market-matching investment strategies that involve minimal turnover and expense. Turnover typically occurs only to accommodate inflows or outflows of investor funds and to improve the market-matching features of the investment portfolio. Also known as index investing.

Ponzi scheme
A type of scam named after the fraudster Charles Ponzi who in the 1920s defrauded thousands of New England residents with the promise of superlative returns on their savings by exploiting anomalies in the rates of exchange offered on international mail coupons. A Ponzi scheme is an investment

fraud that offers the promise of enticing performance by diverting cash from new investors to provide the promised returns to exiting old investors. Such a scheme is doomed to fail and works only as long as new inflows at least match the demand for cash from leavers.

Prepayment risk | The risk that a bond, particularly a mortgage bond, will experience faster than scheduled repayments of principal because residential mortgage holders, particularly in the United States, can exercise the right to repay mortgages earlier than specified in a repayment schedule. This reduces the term of a mortgage bond and is most likely to happen when interest rates fall (or when mortgage providers compete aggressively for new business), giving profitable opportunities for borrowers to remortgage property at more attractive interest rates. See Chapter 9.

Price/earnings ratio | The ratio of a company's share price to its earnings divided by the number of shares it has issued. A high price/earnings (p/e) ratio indicates that the stock market expects the company's earnings to grow fast, and vice versa.

Price performance | The performance of an investment that makes no allowance for its income or dividend yield. Contrast with total return, which includes the price performance and the income return.

Private investment | An unlisted or unquoted investment for which price quotations are generally not readily available.

Private equity	Funds or investors that directly buy private companies, or that engage in buy-outs of public companies, with high fee charges and restrictive redemption terms.
Prospect theory	A key part of behavioural finance. It is based on experiments that indicate that people are more motivated by losses than by gains and so will try hard to avoid realising losses. See Chapter 2.
Public market or quoted investment	A listed or quoted investment for which prices are regularly quoted on a formal exchange at which, or close to which, transactions can be effected. See **unlisted investment**.
Real interest rate	The rate of interest after allowing for inflation.
Risk premium	Several risk premia are discussed in Chapter 4.
Safe harbour	An investor's minimum-risk strategy. See Chapter 4.
Sharpe ratio	A measure of risk-adjusted performance. measured as the ratio of performance in excess of the risk-free investment (generally Treasury bills) to the volatility of performance relative to the risk-free rate. Performance and volatility are generally calculated as annualised rates. Investors should be aware that illiquid investment strategies distort measurement of Sharpe ratios, since the apparent volatility of those strategies will be artificially reduced by markets that rely on appraisal valuations of underlying investments. Sharpe ratios are only meaningful if the distribution of performance of the underlying investments approximately resembles a normal distribution. It follows that Sharpe ratios should not be used for investment strategies which resemble

insurance programmes and which incorporate a marked degree of optionality. For both these reasons, Sharpe ratios shown for many hedge fund strategies are more likely to misinform investors than to inform them. See Chapter 4.

Short position   Arises when investors sell an investment that they do not own. Unless the short position is established on a futures exchange, investors will need to borrow the investment to deliver it to the counterparty who bought it from them. The short seller will need to provide collateral to the stock lender when borrowing the stock (or other investment). In contrast, a long position is an investment which is owned.

Small cap   A smaller company by stock market capitalisation. In the United States a common definition is that a quoted company is small cap if its market capitalisation is less than $2 billion. See Chapter 8.

Sovereign wealth fund (SWF)   A government-owned investment fund, typically arising from persistent balance-of-payments surpluses.

Stable coins   Cryptocurrencies whose value is pegged, or backed by other fiat currencies, commodities or financial instruments. They are often regarded as crypto-friendly substitutes for money market funds, but regulators worry about the absence of transparency on assets backing them and use of leverage.

SPAC   Special purpose acquisition company, or a blank-cheque company. See Chapter 8.

Standard deviation	Standard deviation of returns measures the dispersion about the mean (or average) return.
Stocks	The same as equities or shares.
Stock selection	The allocation of investments in a portfolio within a particular market. Contrast with the allocation of investments among different markets, which is known as asset allocation.
Strategic asset allocation	Decisions, typically intended to be long term in nature, to manage risks and opportunities relative to an investor's ultimate payment obligations or objectives. Strategic asset allocation involves the allocation of investments between an investor's safe-harbour investment and risky investments that represent an efficient diversity of other market risks. See Chapters 5 and 6.
Structured product	An investment or investment strategy that is typically sold with some element of principal protection and/or of leverage to give accelerated exposure to the underlying market. Structured products are sold by investment banks and typically involve either (i) some combination of zero coupon bonds, which mature with the structured product, together with call options on the relevant underlying market; or (ii) a dynamic strategy that adjusts exposure to the underlying investment and government bonds to ensure that the issuing bank will be able profitably to honour the promised capital repayment at maturity.
Sub-investment or speculative grade	A debt issue judged by credit-rating agencies to be at best speculative or not well secured. See also **high-yield bond**, **investment grade** and Chapter 9.

Systematic return	The market return that is expected to be provided for bearing well-diversified systematic risk. Often thought of in terms of equity market return, systematic return also refers to the return that should be expected for bearing any type of market risk for which market participants are willing to pay. This includes, in addition to equity market risk, credit market risk, as well as various types of insurance and other risk transfer services. Such alternative sources of systematic return are now understood to be an important potential source of hedge fund returns.
Systematic risk	The market risk that remains after diversification. Most commonly this refers to equity market risk, but it can also refer to the risk associated with a range of different sources of systematic return.
Tactical opportunities	Opportunities to profit from expected short-term differential performance between markets by allocating more or less of an investment strategy to different markets.
Total return	The total performance of an investment, combining income yield as well as price performance.
Tranche	A slice, specifically of a collateralised debt obligation (CDO), that has different risk characteristics from other tranches of the same CDO. See Chapter 9.
Treasury bill	Government debt with less than one year's original maturity (typically between one and six months).

Treasury bond	Government debt with more than one year's original maturity. In designing broad investment strategies, it is conventional to treat a government bond with a remaining maturity of less than 12 months as if it were a Treasury bill. In the United States, Treasury debts with between one and ten years' original maturity are called "notes". In this book, "Treasury bond" refers to any Treasury security of more than one year's maturity.
Unhedged	An indication that market risk, for example from the stock market or a foreign exchange market, has not been neutralised using derivatives or other instruments.
Unlisted or private investment	An investment, such as a venture capital investment or a property investment, the price of which, except when it is bought and sold, represents appraisal valuations.
Utility	An indication of satisfaction, often proxied by money.
Venture capital	A type of private equity investment focused on start-up companies and small businesses with long-term growth potential.
Volatility	Fluctuations in the price or performance of an investment, typically measured by the annualised standard deviation of returns.
Yield curve	See Chapter 4.

Notes

Introduction
1. The anecdote that starts the chapter is borrowed from Brett and Marcos Talk Your Chart, US Market Domination & 2022 Predictions, episode 11 webcast, Evensky & Katz/Foldes: www.evensky.com

Chapter 1. Where's the beef?
1. Ilmanen, A., *Expected Returns: An Investor's Guide to Harvesting Market Rewards* (John Wiley & Sons, 2011).
2. See, for example, the Money Tales series of books for children written by Sheila Bair, former head of the US Federal Deposit Insurance Corporation.
3. Ludwig, C., "The myth of full automation: the roboadvice case", Bank Underground, Bank of England staff blog (January 2020).

Chapter 2. "Know thyself": can I trust my own advice or do I need an adviser?
1. Dimson, E., P. Marsh and M. Staunton, *Credit Suisse Global Investment Returns Yearbook 2021* (Credit Suisse Research Institute/London Business School, 2021), summary edition, p.27.
2. Finance academics call this demand for lottery tickets (and for investments with lottery type characteristics) a preference for positive skewness.

Chapter 3. The personal pension challenge
1. Chen, G., M. Lee and T. Nam, "Forced retirement risk and portfolio choice", *Journal of Empirical Finance* 58(C) (2020). The article examines US data collected in annual surveys of the elderly from 1998 to 2012 by the University of Michigan's Health and Retirement Study.

2. Ezra, D., "Most people need longevity insurance rather than an immediate annuity", *Financial Analysts Journal* 72(2) (2016).
3. "The challenge of longevity risk: making retirement income last a lifetime", American Academy of Actuaries, Institute and Faculty of Actuaries, Actuaries Institute Australia (2015).
4. Hurd, M.D., P.-C. Michaud and S. Rohwedder, "Distribution of lifetime nursing home use and out-of-pocket spending", Rand Corporation and Network for Studies on Pension, Aging and Retirement, Tilburg University (2017).
5. Bengen, W.P., "Determining withdrawal rates using historical data", *Journal of Financial Planning* 7(4) (1994).
6. Maeso, J.-M. et al., "Efficient withdrawal strategies in retirement investing", EDHEC-Risk Institute (March 2022).
7. Horneff, V., R. Maurer and O.S. Mitchell, "Putting the pension back in 401(k) retirement plans: optimal versus default deferred longevity income annuities", *Journal of Banking & Finance* 114 (2020).

Chapter 4. What drives performance?

1. Academic studies from different countries have shown underperformance of the broad market and often negative returns from day trading. These studies include the following.

    Barber, B.M. et al., "Attention-induced trading and returns: evidence from Robinhood users", SSRN mimeo (October 2021).

    A much earlier US study highlighted underperformance of the broad market by day traders: Barber, B.M. and T. Odean, "Trading is hazardous to your wealth: the common stock investment performance of individual investors", *Journal of Finance* 55(2) (2000).

    A third example, from Brazil, is Chaque, F., R. De-Losso and B. Giovannetti, "Day trading for a living?", SSRN mimeo (June 2020). The researchers studied trading by individuals in the Brazilian equity futures market between 2013 and 2015. They found that 97% who persisted for at least 300 days lost money and that only 1.1% earned more than the Brazilian minimum wage.
2. Bessembinder, H., "Do stocks outperform Treasury bills", *Journal of Financial Economics* (September 2018).
3. Vlieghe, G., "The yield curve and QE", speech given at the Imperial College Business School, September 2018 (accessed from bankofengland.co.uk); and P. Tucker "On central bank independence", *Finance and Development*, IMF (May 2020).

4. Dimson, E., P. Marsh and M. Staunton, *Credit Suisse Global Investment Returns Yearbook 2022* (Credit Suisse Research Institute/London Business School, 2022). This updates E. Dimson, P. Marsh and M. Staunton, *Triumph of the Optimists: 101 Years of Global Investment Returns* (Princeton University Press, 2002).
5. As a result, UK real interest rates, on an internationally comparable basis, have been materially higher, and the break-even rates of inflation materially lower, than shown by the published data.

Chapter 5. Inflation, interest rates, booms and busts: is anything safe?

1. Summers, L.H., "The age of secular stagnation: what it is and what to do about it", *Foreign Affairs* (March/April 2016).
2. Mayer, T. and G. Schnabl, "Reasons for the demise of interest: savings glut, and secular stagnation or central bank policy?", *Quarterly Journal of Austrian Economics* 24(1) (2021).
3. Buiter, W.H., "Gold: a six thousand year old bubble revisited", Citi Economics Research paper (2014), www.willembuiter.com/gold2.pdf
4. Rogoff, K.S., *The Curse of Cash* (Princeton University Press, 2016).
5. The last vestiges of this formal role were finally dismantled in 1971 when the USA ended the facility for central banks to exchange dollars for gold at $35 per troy ounce.
6. The largest denomination banknotes in circulation in 2022 were $100 in the US, £50 in the UK, and €500 in the euro zone. The €500 note has not been issued since 2019, but it was still legal tender in 2022.
7. Nakamoto, S., "Bitcoin: a peer-to-peer electronic cash system", (October 2008).
8. Turpin, J.B., "Bitcoin: the economic case for a global, virtual currency operating in an unexplored legal framework", *Indiana Journal of Global Legal Studies* 335 (2014).
9. "The future monetary system". Speech by Hyun Song Shin to the BIS Annual General Meeting, June 2022.
10. Aliber, R.Z., C.P. Kindleberger and R.N. McCauley, *Manias, Panics and Crashes: A History of Financial Crises* (Wiley, 8th edn, 2022).
11. Shiller, R.J., *Irrational Exuberance* (Princeton University Press, 2000).
12. Goetzmann, W.N., "Bubble investing: learning from history", in Chambers, D. and E. Dimson (eds) *Financial Market History: Reflections on the Past for Investors Today* (CFA Institute Research Foundation and University of Cambridge Judge Business School, 2016).
13. Quinn, W. and J.D. Turner, *Boom and Bust: A Global History of Financial Bubbles* (Cambridge University Press, 2020).

14. The Shiller PE is the ratio of the inflation-adjusted level of the S&P composite stock price index to the inflation-adjusted ten-year moving average of the reported earnings of the companies in the index.

Chapter 6. Will model allocations help me invest better?

1. Tobin, J., "Liquidity preference as behaviour towards risk", *Review of Economic Studies* 67 (1958).
2. In the UK, the savings bank Northern Rock was rescued by the Bank of England in September 2007 following a dramatic, televised run of depositor withdrawals in 2007. In September 2008, following the bankruptcy of Lehman Brothers, the leading US money market fund, the $65 billion Reserve Primary Fund, was forced to mark its unit value below $1.00, triggering a flood of redemption requests. In turn this led to a US Treasury Temporary Guarantee Program for money market funds.
3. Siegel, J.J., *Stocks for the Long Run* (McGraw-Hill, 5th edn, 2014).

Chapter 7. Liquidity risk: in bad times, cash is king

1. Johnson, E. and D. Moggridge (eds), *The Collected Writings of John Maynard Keynes, Vol. XII, Investment and Editorial* (Royal Economic Society, 1978), p.108.
2. Ibid., p.109.
3. In 2021, the UK introduced a framework for a new category of fund for illiquid investments called a long-term asset fund. Redemptions are to be no more frequent than monthly and then after a minimum 90-day notice period.

Chapter 8. Risk assets: global equity markets

1. By the end of 2020, more than $15 trillion was invested in index-tracking mutual funds and exchange traded funds of equities and bonds, according to the Investment Company Institute. These are enormous sums.
2. Source: Investment Company Institute, "Profile of mutual fund shareholders, 2020".
3. In the UK, the consultancy Tumelo encourages fund managers to collect the opinions of their unitholders on issues ahead of AGM votes and to reflect those opinions in how they vote their funds' shares.
4. Source: Dimson, E., P. Marsh and M. Staunton, *Credit Suisse Global Investment Returns Yearbook 2021* (Credit Suisse Research Institute/ London Business School, 2021).

5. For an academic assessment of underdiversification, see Campbell, J.Y., *Financial Decisions and Markets: A Course in Asset Pricing* (Princeton University Press, 2018), pp.323–31.
6. Campbell, J.Y., K. Serfaty-de Medeiros and L.M. Viceira, "Global currency hedging", *Journal of Finance* 65(1) (2010).
7. An easy test is to compare the **correlation** of domestic and international equities with domestic government bonds. The home bias might be justified if domestic equities correlate better than international equities with domestic bonds. In practice, this does not provide ready evidence to support moving far away from a diversified global approach to investing in equities for a European, UK or US investor. Researchers have examined much more sophisticated arguments, including correlations with domestic labour costs, and with domestic inflation, to justify a home-country bias in equity strategies. But the results are not conclusive.
8. This is represented by the largest 10% of listed domestic companies in the stock price database of the University of Chicago's Center for Research in Security Prices.

Chapter 9. Risk assets: global credit

1. Corporate bonds should be expected to underperform government debt in bad times because of the financial options that are implicit within credit. This insight, which flows from the pioneering work of Nobel prize-winning economist Robert Merton and colleagues in the early 1970s, helps to demonstrate how corporate bonds perform in different environments. Normally, the investor in the corporate bond gets a reward equivalent to the return on the government bond, plus the premium which is paid to the investor in return for the option (or insurance) that bond investors grant or sell to the firm's creditors. Seen in this way, the option is not needed, and so is worthless if the company survives and can repay the corporate bond in full at maturity. The link between option pricing and the stock market results in an important close relationship between stock market volatility and the performance of corporate bond funds. When stock market volatility increases, we should expect the performance of corporate bond funds to be disappointing.
2. Giesecke, K. et al., "Corporate bond default risk: a 150-year perspective", *Journal of Financial Economics* 102(2) (2011).
3. Ilmanen, A., *Expected Returns: An Investor's Guide to Harvesting Market Rewards* (Wiley, 2011); Ng, K.-Y. and B.D. Phelps, "Capturing the credit spread premium", *Financial Analysts Journal* 67(3) (2011).

4. As in developed countries, emerging market bonds are predominantly issued in local currencies, with China alone representing 53% of all outstanding emerging market bonds in mid-2022. Chinese bond issuance is closely connected to government sponsored funding and government institutions issue most of the debt, which in turn is mostly held by Chinese banks.

5. W.N. Goetzmann, Edwin J. Beinecke Professor of Finance at Columbia Business School, provides a very readable account of the mass marketing of skyscraper bonds during the 1920s and their subsequent collapse in value in *Money Changes Everything: How Finance Made Civilization Possible* (Princeton University Press, 2016) pp.477–81.

6. Derman, E. *Models. Behaving. Badly. Why Confusing Illusion with Reality Can Lead to Disaster on Wall Street and in Life* (Wiley, 2011).

7. The discussion of quantitative investment and the global financial crisis draws on an article by F. Salmon "Recipe for disaster: the formula that killed Wall Street", *Wired Magazine* (February 2009) and also C. Reavis, "The global financial crisis of 2008: the role of greed, fear and oligarchs", *MIT Sloan School of Management* (2009).

Chapter 10. Multi-asset funds and alternative investments

1. Investors can now acquire diversified exposure to the private debt market by investing in a private credit exchange traded fund. As with any market subject to illiquidity, investors in an ETF should satisfy themselves that the managers of the ETF will be able to balance the apparent liquidity mismatch between a traded ETF and any illiquidity of the underlying market.

2. Phalippou, L., "An inconvenient fact: private equity returns and the billionaire factory", *Journal of Investing* 30(1) (2020).

Chapter 11. Home ownership and real estate

1. Source: UN Environment Programme, *2019 Global Status Report for Buildings and Construction*.

2. According to real estate consultancy SMR Research, the average US commercial building was 53 years old in 2021.

3. Hoesli, M. and E. Oikarinen, "Does listed real estate behave like direct real estate? Updated and broader evidence", *Applied Economics* 53(26) (2021); Lizieri, C., S. Satchell and W. Wongwachara, "Unsmoothing real estate returns: a regime-switching approach", *Real Estate Economics* 40(4) (2012), pp.775–807.

Chapter 12. Art and investments of passion

1. Reitlinger, G., *The Economics of Taste: The Rise and Fall of Picture Prices 1760–1960* (Barrie and Rockliff, 1961). Reitlinger says that at the time (1808) the £12,600 paid for the two Claudes had only ever been exceeded by the £8,500 paid for Raphael's Sistine Madonna in 1754.
2. Mei, J. and M. Moses, "Art as an investment and the underperformance of masterpieces", *American Economic Review* 92(5) (2002).
3. Leading auction houses filter the art that is offered at their auctions. They naturally want their auctions to succeed. This makes it more likely that auctions represent individual styles and artists that are currently in fashion and so unlikely to be undervalued. In addition, an auction is likely to incorporate more (possibly all) available information on the price of an asset than a valuer's valuation, which will always seek to catch up with current market conditions. For these reasons, buying art at auction is unlikely to be rewarded consistently with superior price performance. Academic research seems to confirm this.
4. See the section on the obsolescence of art in Grampp, W.D., *Pricing the Priceless: Art, Artists and Economics* (Basic Books, 1989), Chapter 2.
5. Source: Christie's, www.christies.com/features/nft-101-collection-guide-to-nft-11654–7.aspx
6. Source: The Art Market 2022, Arts Economics for Art Basel and UBS.
7. Goetzmann, W.N., L. Renneboog and C. Spaenjers, "Art and money", *American Economic Review* 101(3) (2011), pp. 222–6.
8. Grampp, W.D., *Pricing the Priceless: Art, Artists and Economics* (Basic Books, 1989).
9. Pownall, R., S. Satchell and N. Srivastava, *The Estimation of Psychic Returns from Cultural Assets*, mimeo, 2013.
10. Ginsburgh, V. and S. Weyers, "Persistence and fashion in art: Italian Renaissance from Vasari to Berenson and beyond", *Poetics* 34(1) (2006).
11. The fable is that van Gogh sold only two paintings. We do not know how many he sold, but it was more than two. The website of the Van Gogh Museum in Amsterdam gives some background: www.vangoghmuseum.nl
12. Landes, W.M., "Winning the art lottery: the economic returns to the Ganz Collection", *Louvain Economic Review* 66(2) (2000).
13. According to Artprice.com the unsold rate at fine art auctions in 2021 was 31%.
14. McAndrew, C. and R. Thompson, "The collateral value of fine art", *Journal of Banking and Finance* 31(3) (2007), pp. 589–607.

Further reading

Chapter 1. Where's the beef?

Brayman, S. and J. Stipp, "Measurement of client risk tolerance: How improving methodology could offer advisors a significant competitive advantage", Morningstar, 2021.

Kahneman, D., "The myth of risk attitudes", *Journal of Portfolio Management* 36(1) (2009).

Kay, J. and M. King, *Radical Uncertainty: Decision-Making Beyond the Numbers* (Norton, 2020).

Klapper, L. and A. Lusardi, "Financial literacy and financial resilience: evidence from around the world", *Financial Management* 49(3) (2019).

Mitchell, O.S. and A. Lusardi, "Financial literacy and financial behavior at older ages", Global Financial Literacy Excellence Center, WP 2021–3 (July 2021).

Chapter 2. Know thyself: can I trust my own advice or do I need an adviser?

Akerlof, G.A., "Behavioral macroeconomics and macroeconomic behavior". Nobel prize lecture (November 2001): www.nobelprize.org

Kahneman, D., *Thinking, Fast and Slow* (Farrar, Straus and Giroux, 2011).

Lo, A., *Adaptive Markets: Financial Evolution at the Speed of Thought* (Princeton University Press, 2017).

Chapter 3. The personal pension challenge

Scott, J.S., W.F. Sharpe and J.G. Watson, "The 4% rule – at what price?", *Journal of Investment Management* 7(3) (2009).

Chapter 4. What drives investment performance?

Damodaran, A., "Equity risk premiums (ERP): determinants, estimation and implications – the 2022 edition": stern.nyu.edu

Damodaran, A., *Investment Fables: Exposing the Myth of 'Can't Miss' Investment Strategies* (Financial Times/Prentice Hall, 2004).

Dimson, E., P. Marsh and M. Staunton, *Credit Suisse Global Investment Returns Yearbook 2022* (Credit Suisse Research Institute/London Business School, 2022).

Dimson, E., P. Marsh and M. Staunton, *Triumph of the Optimists: 101 Years of Global Investment Returns* (Princeton University Press, 2002).

Harvey, C.R., "Be skeptical of asset management research", SSRN (2021): ssrn.com/abstract=3906277

Ibbotson, R.G. and J.P. Harrington, *Stocks, Bonds, Bills and Inflation: 2021 Summary Edition,* Morningstar (CFA Institute Research Foundation and Duff & Phelps, 2021).

Ilmanen, A., *Investing Amid Low Expected Returns* (Wiley, 2022).

Ilmanen, A., *Expected Returns: An Investor's Guide to Harvesting Market Rewards* (John Wiley & Sons, 2011).

Chapter 5. Inflation, interest rates, booms and busts: is anything safe?

Allen, H.J., "DeFi: shadow banking 2.0?", *William and Mary Law Review* (2022).

Bernstein, P.L., *The Power of Gold: The History of an Obsession*, (Wiley, 2nd edn, 2012).

Buiter, W.H., "Gold: a six thousand year bubble revisited", Citi Economics Research paper (2014), www.willembuiter.com/gold2.pdf

Deutsche Bundesbank, *Germany's Gold* (Hirmer, 2019).

Erb, C.B. and C.R. Harvey, "The golden dilemma", *Financial Analysts Journal* 69(4) (2013).

Financial Stability Board, *Assessment of Risks to Financial Stability from Crypto-assets*, Bank for International Settlements (February 2022).

Goodhart, C. and M. Pradhan, *The Great Demographic Reversal: Ageing Societies, Waning Inequality, and an Inflation Revival* (Palgrave Macmillan, 2020).

International Monetary Fund, "Chapter 2. The crypto ecosystem and financial stability challenges", *Global Financial Stability Report, October 2021* (2021).

Makarov, I. and A. Schoar, "Blockchain analysis of the bitcoin market", NBER working paper 29396 (2021).

Quinn, W. and J.D. Turner, *Boom and Bust: A Global History of Financial Bubbles* (Cambridge University Press, 2020).

Summers, L.H., "The age of secular stagnation: what it is and what to do about it", *Foreign Affairs* (March/April 2016).

World Gold Council website (www.gold.org) is a mine of useful information and statistics on gold.

Chapter 6. Will model allocations help me invest better?

Ang, A., "Illiquid assets", *CFA Institute Conference Proceedings Quarterly* 28(4) (2011).

Capgemini Research Institute, *The World Wealth Report*, 2022.

Rogoff, K.S., *The Curse of Cash* (Princeton University Press, 2016).

Salmon, F., "Recipe for disaster: the formula that killed Wall Street", *Wired Magazine* (February 2009).

Chapter 7. Liquidity risk: in bad times, cash is king

Ang, A., *Asset Management: A Systematic Approach to Factor Investing* (Oxford University Press, 2014).

Asness, C., "The illiquidity discount?", AQR perspective (2019).

Johnson, E. and D. Moggridge (eds), *The Collected Writings of John Maynard Keynes, Vol. XII, Investment and Editorial* (Royal Economic Society, 1978).

Chapter 8. Risk assets: global equity markets

Anson, M. et al., "The sustainability conundrum", *Journal of Portfolio Management* (March 2020).

Arnott, R.D. et al., "Alice's adventures in factorland: three blunders that plague factor investing", *Journal of Portfolio Management* (April 2019).

Arnott, R.D. et al., "Reports of value's death may be greatly exaggerated", *Financial Analysts Journal* 77(1) (2021).

Bebchuk, L.A. and S. Hirst, "Index funds and the future of corporate governance: theory, evidence and policy", *Columbia Law Review* 119 (2019).

Bebchuk, L.A. and S. Hirst, "The specter of the giant three", *Boston University Law Review* 99 (2019).

Campbell, J.Y., K. Serfaty-de Medeiros and L.M. Viceira, "Global currency hedging", *Journal of Finance* 65(1) (2010).

Dasgupta, P., *The Economics of Biodiversity: The Dasgupta Review*, (HM Treasury, 2021).

Eccles, R.G. and S. Klimenko, "The investor revolution", *Harvard Business Review* (May/June 2019).

Fisch, J.E., "Mutual fund stewardship and the empty voting problem", *Faculty Scholarship at Penn Carey Law* 2678 (2021).

Florentsen, B. et al., "The aggregate cost of equity underdiversification", *Financial Review* 55(1) (2019).

Kavour, A., "Equity home bias: a review essay", *Journal of Economic Surveys* 33(3) (2020).

Lee, A.H., "Every vote counts: the importance of fund voting and disclosure", speech at the 2021 ICI Mutual Funds and Investment Management Conference.

Lochstoer, L.A. and P.C. Tetlock, "What drives anomaly returns?", *Journal of Finance* 75(3) (2020).

Schneider, P., C. Wagner and J. Zechner, "Low-risk anomalies?", *Journal of Finance* 75(5) (2020).

Somerset Webb, M., *Share Power: How Ordinary People Can Change the Way that Capitalism Works – and Make Money Too* (Short Books, 2022).

World Bank Group, *Purchasing Power Parities and the Size of World Economies: Results from the 2017 International Comparison Program* (World Bank, 2020).

Chapter 9. Risk assets: global credit

Aramonte, S. and F. Avalos, "Corporate credit markets after the initial pandemic shock", *BIS Bulletin* 26 (2020).

Giesecke, K. et al., "Corporate bond default risk: a 150-year perspective", *Journal of Financial Economics* 102(2) (2011).

Chapter 10. Multi-asset funds and alternative investments

Blake, D. and D. Harrison, "And death shall have no dominion: life settlements and the ethics of profiting from mortality", Pensions Institute, Cass Business School (2008).

Böni, P. and S. Manigart, "Private debt fund returns and general partner skills", Tilburg University (2021).

Gregoriou, G.N. and F-S. Lhabitant, "Madoff: A Riot of Red Flags", EDHEC Risk and Asset Management Research Centre (2009).

Harris, R.S., T. Jenkinson and S.N. Kaplan, "How do private equity investments perform compared to public equity?", *Journal of Investment Management* (2016).

Jorion, P., "Hedge funds vs. alternative risk premia", *Financial Analysts Journal* 77(4) (2021).

Lester, K. and F. Scheepers, "Risk in private debt", Validus Risk Management (2014).

Neureuter, J., "The institutional digital investor assets study", Fidelity Investments (2021).

Phalippou, L., "An inconvenient fact: private equity returns and the billionaire factory", *Journal of Investing* 30(1) (2020).

Preqin, *2021 Preqin Global Private Debt Report* (2021).

Chapter 11. Home ownership and real estate

Hoesli, M. and E. Oikarinen, "Does listed real estate behave like direct real estate? Updated and broader evidence", *Applied Economics* 53(26) (2021).

Lizieri C., S. Satchell and W. Wongwachara, "Unsmoothing real estate returns: a regime-switching approach", *Real Estate Economics* 40(4) (2012).

Preqin, *2021 Preqin Global Private Debt Report* (2021).

UN Environment Programme, *2019 Global Status Report for Buildings and Construction*.

Chapter 12. Art and investments of passion

Baumol, W.J., "Unnatural value or art as a floating crap game", *American Economic Review* 76(2) (1986).

Deloitte & ArtTactic, *Art & Finance Report 2021*, 7th edn (2021).

Ginsburgh, V. and S. Weyers, "Persistence and fashion in art: Italian Renaissance from Vasari to Berenson and beyond", *Poetics* 34(1) (2006).

Grampp, W.D., *Pricing the Priceless: Art, Artists and Economics* (Basic Books, 1989).

McAndrew, C., *Art Market 2021, The Art Basel & UBS Global Art Market Report*, 5th edn (2021).

Reitlinger, G., *The Economics of Taste: The Rise and Fall of Picture Prices 1760–1960* (Barrie and Rockliff, 1961).

Acknowledgements

We owe a debt of gratitude to many individuals who helped with this book. First and foremost to our wives, Alex, Ana and Rubina for their continued support and patience through this book's long gestation. Very notably, Jayaraman Rajakumar provided skilled and extensive research assistance, which has proved invaluable. Generous and insightful contributions on particular issues or chapters were provided by Chris Bartram, Elroy Dimson, Hugh Ferry, Hamzah Javaid, Mike Lea, Colin Lizieri, Tim Lund, Mark Ralphs, Oliver Stanyer, Richard Williams, Oliver Williams and Esmond James Wyatt. We are most grateful to each of them, but any mistakes are our own. We would also like to thank Clare Grist Taylor at Profile Books for her encouragement and many wise suggestions. These have been most helpful. We would also like to thank Philippa Logan for her patient and skilled editing of our book, and Paul Forty for his good-natured supervision of the editorial work.

This book aims to help inform investors about investing. It does not give recommendations on whether to buy or sell specific investments. It draws on and summarises research and investor perspectives on a wide range of issues. It has some notes citing sources, but these do not pretend to be comprehensive. Although important areas of debate are flagged with references to leading researchers, in other areas ideas that are more commonly expressed are presented.

Sources that were particularly important for each chapter are listed in the Notes and Further Reading sections.

Please note that the views expressed in this book are our own and may not coincide with the views of the investment funds or other bodies on whose boards or committees we have been honoured to serve and advise.

Peter Stanyer, peter@peterstanyer.com
Masood Javaid, how_to_invest@hotmail.com
Stephen Satchell, ses11@cam.ac.uk

Index

References to figures, tables, and other illustrative material are shown in *italics*